LOS ANGELES
BEFORE THE FREEWAYS

Felipe de Neve in the Plaza

Once, the statue of Felipe de Neve—who founded El Pueblo de la Reina de Los Angeles—stood perched on a granite boulder in the middle of a fountain pool, at the center of the Plaza. Today, the eight-foot bronze statue, sculpted by Henry Lion and erected by the Native Daughters of the Golden West in 1932, has been shunted off to the side of the Plaza, and has had his back turned to the church, rather than facing it.

LOS ANGELES
BEFORE THE FREEWAYS

IMAGES OF AN ERA 1850–1950

Arnold Hylen with Nathan Marsak

For Gustaf M. Hylen and Anna E. Hylen, née Birath

— *Arnold Hylen*

To documentarians everywhere

— *Nathan Marsak*

Hildreth Mansion: Victorian ornamentation
The Hildreth home at 357 S. Hope St. was designed by Joseph Cather Newsom, utilizing all of Newsom's signature Queen Anne architectural flourishes. The house languished for decades before it was purchased in 1946 by John and Mable Haufe, who restored and renamed it "Hopecrest." The city took it from them in 1953 via eminent domain, and demolished the house as part of construction of the Fourth Street cut, a viaduct that sliced through Bunker Hill, funneling traffic from the new Harbor Freeway into downtown.

Overleaf: The view south on Third Street, across Fremont Avenue
The church was built as a Quaker Friends Church, and dedicated in March 1901. It was demolished in 1950. Everything in this image has been demolished, save for the west entrance to the Third Street Tunnel.

A NOTE ON THE TEXT

The first edition of *Los Angeles Before the Freeways* was published in 1981 by Dawson's Book Shop. Hylen's essay and photographs are republished in this updated edition with expanded captions by Nathan Marsak that provide additional context for each image. Hylen's text is presented as it was originally published in 1981.

Den's Building: the Italianate façade
Built of brick, stone, and iron, the Downey Block at 330 N. Main St. (page 71) was a tour de force of High Victorian Italianate, with its swan's neck pediment and heavily framed window surrounds. C.W. Davis's earlier block for John G. Downey at Temple and Main, built in 1871 (demolished 1904) had been a more faithful version of the Renaissance Revival.

CONTENTS

First Los Angeles High School: Fort Moore Hill
This Italianate-style school (Ezra F. Kysor, 1873) was lifted onto a tall rolling platform in 1886 and (after getting stuck high above Temple Street and proving immovable for months) was relocated to Sand Street on Fort Moore Hill, to facilitate construction of the county courthouse.

Overleaf: Southwest corner of First and Flower
The four flats at 101–111 S. Flower St. were built in the spring of 1904 by contractor and former City Councilman Frank Walker, who lived in a large house across the street on the southeast corner. (The low wall where the people are walking bordered his home.)

INTRODUCTION

Nathan Marsak

In the 1950s, documenting *old* Los Angeles was something of a revolutionary act. The postwar Southland was at the forefront of everything new, shiny, and futuristic. Southern California was a place of gleaming modern highways, shuttling rocket-finned autos from suburban tract homes to sprawling shopping centers. Los Angeles was at the vanguard of the aerospace industry, had pioneered fast-food restaurants, and its coffee shops were bold space-age parabolas of glass and steel. Few shed a tear for the disappearing world of weird wooden houses and creaky, cast-iron commercial structures.

Those who did probably seemed anachronistic in this new world of clean lines and pathological forward-thinking. One such anachronism was Arnold Hylen, a quiet and unassuming man with a fancy for Los Angeles's complex and picturesque past.

Gustav Arnold Hylen—known throughout his life as Arnold—was born August 7, 1908 in Kristinehamn, Sweden to Gustaf Manfred Hylen, a carpenter, and Anna Elisabet (Birath) Hylen. The Hylen family emigrated to America soon after his birth, departing Liverpool on the RMS *Mauretania* and arriving in New York May 21, 1909. They settled in Proctor, Vermont.

In 1917, the family relocated to California, moving first to Redondo Beach, then to the Harvard Park neighborhood of south Los Angeles. In 1924, sixteen-year-old Arnold was accepted to the Chouinard Art Institute. By age nineteen, he was a dedicated artist. Hylen entered and was lauded in exhibitions; his painting *Sensation*, a portrait of a girl, was complimented by the *Los Angeles Times* in a review of the 1928 Los Angeles Museum Exhibition of Painters and Sculptors. But the Depression hit and Hylen went back to Vermont, having secured gainful employment

Hylen leans against a storefront in the Martz Flats (page 170), ca. 1955.

designing monuments at the marble works. He returned to Los Angeles when his mother died in 1937 and lived with his sister and widowed father in Hollywood.

Hylen was kept out of service in World War II due to his high myopia, so he found employment at the Fluor Corporation, an oil and gas engineering and construction company. He photographed oil refineries, designed and produced sales brochures, and arranged exhibits for trade shows. It was during this time he became interested in photographing old Los Angeles. After a long week, on Sunday mornings he'd set out for downtown from his home in Boyle Heights and spend the day walking the streets, camera in hand, which fed his interest in the fast-disappearing downtown area, Bunker Hill in particular.

One of Hylen's pictures was used in Tom Atwill Neal's eleven-page book *St. Vibiana's Los Angeles Cathedral*, published in 1950. In 1968 Hylen produced an eight-page folio *The Vanishing Face of Los Angeles*. Both were published by Dawson's Book Shop.

After his retirement from Fluor in 1973, encouraged by his friend the bookseller and publisher Glen Dawson, Hylen began work putting together books filled with the images he'd shot over the years, accompanied by explanatory text. This resulted in two books published by Dawson's Book Shop: his 1976 *Bunker Hill: A Los Angeles Landmark* and *Los Angeles Before the Freeways 1850-1950: Images of an Era* in 1981.

There was one exhibition of Hylen's photographs during his lifetime. On June 3,

The Talamentes/Santa Cruz adobe
A rare surviving example of Mexican-era Los Angeles (page 58), built in 1835. The pitched roof is a later addition. Hemmed in by auto dealers and billboards, the important house was viewed by mid-century Angelenos as a curious, inconvenient relic.

1987, the California State Library Foundation hosted an exhibit and reception for a display of his work at the Avila Adobe, in the El Pueblo de Los Angeles Historical Monument. Hylen spoke to the assembled crowd about his experiences capturing bygone Los Angeles. Hylen passed away six months later, on December 23. He was cremated and his remains placed in the Freedom Mausoleum in Forest Lawn Memorial Park, Glendale.

ARCHITECTURE IN HYLEN'S LOS ANGELES

*L*os Angeles Before the Freeways is an invaluable compendium of Los Angeles's nineteenth-century architectural landscape, styles once commonly seen in mid-century downtown.

What follows is a brief and general overview of those styles, once familiar and oft encountered, now largely wiped away.

Pre-Industrial Los Angeles

Prior to California's 1850 statehood, houses and commercial buildings were primarily one story and built out of adobe, with wooden plank roofs sealed by a mix of brea and coarse sand. Around these structures ran broad verandas. Sonoratown, north of the Plaza, was once replete with Spanish and Mexican-era structures, but one by one they disappeared. Many were condemned by the city as hazardous, as they had been built with mud floors, outdoor stoves, and no indoor plumbing; they were modified slowly, if at all. Most, though, were simply lost to "progress."

A newly American Los Angeles saw construction of buildings made from kiln-fired brick beginning in 1852, including the first schoolhouse in Los Angeles. But settlement and development were stymied through the 1850s and '60s by cycles of flooding and drought. Los Angeles only began to grow with the completion of Phineas Banning's 1869 railroad between downtown and his docks in Wilmington, which drastically cut the cost of transporting supplies to Los Angeles.

Evolution and the Italianate

Banning's 1869 railroad from San Pedro's harbor made the importation of building materials easier, to be sure, but the completion of the 1876 transcontinental railroad changed the Los Angeles landscape, literally and figuratively. The 1870s and 1880s saw not only the importation of goods, but also the immigration of craftsmen: stair builders, stone masons, carpenters, wood turners, decorative metal workers, and more. Most importantly, it opened Los Angeles up to the nation, increasing its population.

Residential structures evolved from adobe to wood-frame Folk Victorian, often built in an L-shape, with decorated gables and gingerbread millwork on the porches. Many homes and commercial structures included a four-sided gambrel-style mansard roof with large dormers, in emulation of the Second Empire-era French architectural styles (generally seen as an homage to the progressive ideals of Napoleon III; moreover, twenty percent of Los Angeles's population

was of French extraction). The most imposing structure built in Los Angeles was the 1878 Baker Block at Main and Arcadia Streets, an opulent and ornately decorated office building topped with massive French Renaissance towers (and which replaced the Abel Stearns adobe); its cast-iron plate and structural iron façade was shipped in and would have been impossible before the rail line. A late example of a Second Empire-style mansard roof may be seen in the Rochester (page 177).

Italianate forms were also well represented in Los Angeles. The style had its origins in mid-nineteenth-century romanticism, further promulgated by the wealthy who undertook the "grand tour" of Europe, thus inspired by the Italian architecture they encountered. The Italianate had aspirational appeal, via the elegance and grandeur associated with Italian Renaissance architecture, connoting permanence, solidity, and respectability. Residential applications of the Italianate took cues from the Italian farmhouse, and commercial structures appropriated the architectural vocabulary of sixteenth-century Renaissance palaces. The Italianate is exemplified by the 1873 High School (page 127), with its groupings of tall hooded windows, bracketed cornice, and tower.

The classical standard reigned in part due to the popularity of Europe's enormously influential displays at the 1876 Philadelphia Centennial Exposition. America was also under the sway of architectural and social theorists like Andrew Jackson Downing and Alexander Jackson Davis, who promoted the idea that Gothic Revival and the Italianate

Italianate on Main Street
The 1882 Phillips Block (page 92) is a model of rectitude, given a dignified rhythm via the line of round arched windows. They employ keystones in emphatic hood moldings, framed by repeating pilasters, the formal balance of the whole accentuated by a large bracketed cornice.

were the correct methods for building in America. They believed that establishing an American connection to the ideals and aesthetics of classical European civilization would elevate the taste and refinement of the public. Davis's prolific architecture and Downing's pattern-books of Italianate dwellings were not just replete with a timeless beauty, but were intended to enhance the well-being and character of society.

Boom Years and the Bay Window

The year 1884 saw the publication of Helen Hunt Jackson's novel *Ramona*. The book was a bestseller, depicting Southern California as a picturesque, romantic landscape of lush gardens and idyllic missions. Captivated readers flocked to the Southland, abetted by the chamber of commerce, in league with railroad men, tourism promoters, and real estate speculators. It became every Midwesterner's dream to bask in Southern California's life-renewing sunshine. Thousands of potential homeseekers came to town in the mid-1880s via the new Southern Pacific transcontinental railroad, but when in late 1885 the Santa Fe Railroad completed a second line into Los Angeles, it set off a railroad rate war that dropped the trip price precipitously. Boosters encouraged new pioneers to relocate to LA (and sold lots to new transplants). The boom collapsed in 1887,

and though many new residents departed, the foundation had been laid for a strong and prosperous city.

The architectural style known as Eastlake, named after designer and writer Charles Locke Eastlake, was a robust and angular approach. Eastlake's textured surfaces of wood, stone, and brick underscored an emphasis on natural materials, and its intricate woodwork

Right: The Claremont Block
The Claremont Block (page 148) displays its Eastlake influence, via its symmetry, double-height gabled oriel box-bay windows, carved panels, and geometric patterning. Compare to the adjacent Strong Block, whose canted bay windows—and urns and arches and balustrades—step up the bravura. The use of bay windows is sometimes referred to as the "San Francisco Style." That foggy city had little use for grand porches, but did need to maximize light, and thus began the addition of bay windows in earnest in the late sixties.

Opposite: The Westminster at Fourth and Main Streets
The Westminster (page 113) was one of the many large 1880s projects in Los Angeles to feature a profusion of bays, both square and canted. The Westminster's tall arched Italianate windows, French towers, and a classical cornice with corbels and modillions made for a heady revivalist stew appropriate to the Queen Anne era.

and stained glass display a connection to the craftsmanship and aesthetics of the past, in an increasingly industrialized world. Popularized via the 1876 Centennial Exposition, the Eastlake style held sway through the 1880s. Many hotels and business blocks began to be built with gables and multiple bays, and in the Eastlake tradition, a common characteristic was the steeply pitched roof topped with wrought iron cresting, as seen in the Sepúlveda Block (page 76).

Romanesque Revival

In the mid-nineteenth century, massive German immigration brought America the *rundbogenstil*, or "round arch style." The revivalist style, which had its roots in the early-Medieval Romanesque, expressed itself in dark structures of rusticated stone; it became fashionable in Los Angeles, with its many Germans—and brick kilns and proximity to stone quarries—where it subsequently leant a Teutonic feeling of weight, density, and permanence to town. Romanesque Revival is known for round-headed arches, rusticated and quarry-faced ashlar sandstone, towers, grouped piers, and recessed entrances.

An East Coast architect named Henry Hobson Richardson took the Romanesque Revival ball and ran with it, designing in what became known as the "Richardsonian Romanesque." When the Los Angeles County Courthouse was proposed in 1886, that was the style deemed appropriate. Not all Romanesque Revival structures are necessarily "Richardsonian," but the Los

Angeles Courthouse revealed the obvious influence of Richardson's Allegheny Courthouse, begun in 1884. At one point, downtown Los Angeles had twenty-some major examples of the style, though the majority were demolished before Hylen had a chance to photograph them.

The Queen Anne

The Queen Anne emerged from the Eastlake style, similarly influenced by Gothic Revival and Italianate, but unlike Eastlake's more restrained ornamentation and geometric massing, the Queen Anne featured elaborate decoration, irregular rooflines, and asymmetrical façades. The expressive Queen Anne style had its genesis in the 1876 Philadelphia Centennial Exhibition, where Richard Norman Shaw's heavily patterned fair buildings showcased the charm of Elizabethan/Jacobean decoration. As an 1880s American movement, Queen Anne structures benefitted from new technologies: industrialization had made for the development of mass-produced, machine-cut lumber, including the standard-size two-by-four, which was commonly adopted by building codes so as to ensure safety and consistency in construction. The use of the two-by-four (and that other modern wonder, the cheap, mass-produced, machine-made nail) led to the development of "balloon framing," a construction method using lightweight vertical studs to support the structure; balloon-frame construction allowed structures to become more liberated and structurally expressive. Bunker Hill, a

The Willard Block
The Willard Block (page 114) is typical of Romanesque Revival business block façades which could not be seen "in the round." The Romanesque vernacular was relegated to surface treatment involving round arches, and dark, rough-hewn masonry.

residential development immediately west of the downtown area, was home to many large 1880s homes, first of the more stoic Eastlake variety, later of the florid Queen Anne, which blanketed the landscape in porches and towers and a plethora of intricate lathework.

The 1890s and Beyond: New Visions, Tall Buildings

In 1893, two events combined to change the American consciousness. One was the "White City" of the 1893 World's Columbian Exposition. The fair proposed a neoclassicism that abjured once-fashionable Napoleon III Beaux Arts styles in favor of a new emphasis on the Greco-Roman precedent, and the visual language of the Renaissance. The 1893 fair (and later, Buffalo's 1901 Pan-American Exhibition, and the 1904 Louisiana Purchase Exposition in St. Louis) helped cement the style in the public mind as appropriate for expressing a connection to democracy, our foundation in the Enlightenment, and conveying a culturally literate national identity. America thus found a new visual language in classical proportion, symmetrical fenestration, triangular pediments, and fluted columns.

At the same time, the nation was gripped by the Panic of 1893, a severe economic depression which put new building investment on hold for some years. Southern

Queen Anne on Bunker Hill
Hylen sits in front of the Melrose (page 159). It exemplifies all the features a fashionable home builder would require in the late 1880s: irregular massing, multiple gables, many porches, towers, finials, dormers, scrollwork and carving, and variegated shingle, which combine to form an exuberant visual display. Originally an airy cupola topped the central tower, and to the tower's left was a tall chimney of patterned brick.

California was less affected by the crisis than was most of the West Coast, however, and as such many craftsmen and architects relocated south. These included John Parkinson from Seattle and John C. Austin out of San Francisco, two men who left a dramatic impression on Los Angeles.

Through the 1880s, there were few structures over four stories tall, and by the 1890s, early "skyscraper" architecture had yet to develop a cohesive visual language. The five-story Bradbury and the six-story Stimson Block, both of which opened in 1893, featured strong horizontal features; tall buildings were yet to emphasize their verticality. Verticality in tall buildings was aided later in the nineties through an interpretation of the Beaux Arts, whereby taller structures became tripartite in design, to emulate the "base, shaft, capital" structure of a classical column.

Mission Revival

The Mission Revival was born of the enormously influential Texas and California State Buildings at the 1893 World's Fair, which were based on the Franciscan missions

The Stimson Block
The Stimson Block (page 118) was of immense importance to Los Angeles, being the first steel-frame building of its magnitude in the city (Llewellyn Iron Works provided 1200 tons of steel and 350 tons of cast iron). Despite the Stimson's height, its Romanesque detailing of squat arches and deep balconies, along with two heavy horizontal lines of foliated stringcourse, anchor it to the earth. Moreover, its earthy coloring—mottled-buff Roman pressed brick and brown terra-cotta—is a far cry from the gleaming white glazed brick that would clad the height-limit Beaux Arts office buildings lining Spring Street after 1910 (e.g., John Parkinson's Washington Building, built cater-corner to the Stimson in 1912).

of Spanish-era Alta California. Once building picked up after the economic downturn of 1893, the form was deemed appropriate for the Southland, with major examples built in Los Angeles beginning in the late 1890s. Mission was seen as both picturesque and well-suited to the climate, and was popularized by the likes of Helen Hunt Jackson and Charles Fletcher Lummis. The Mission Revival eventually fell out of favor, replaced by other revivalist styles, like Spanish Colonial.

When people seek "old Los Angeles," they invariably head downtown, and marvel at its incredible collection of Beaux Arts commercial structures, built between 1900 and 1925. These blend in well with the large Modernist 1950s projects, like the Court House and the Hall of Records. Most forms of "old LA" have vanished, however.

The Bur-Mar

The Bur-Mar (page 168), built in 1903. A typically Edwardian-era confection of neoclassical elements, with strong bilateral symmetry and a massive pedimented central pavilion of fluted Corinthian columns.

LOS ANGELES BEFORE THE FREEWAYS

Remaining Victorian-era structures are generally of the earliest variety and made all the more anachronistic by being confined to the "historic park" area. Without Hylen's documentation of downtown's erstwhile wonderland of bay windows and turrets, one might not even know that the "High Victorian" forms of Queen Anne and Romanesque once populated the landscape (the last two major bay window structures in central downtown, at 324 and 328 S. Hill St., were demolished by developer Ira Yellin in 1988). Understanding the myriad of forms architecture took in the Victorian era provides insight into the cultural, social, and economic conditions of Los Angeles's evolution, and serves to remind that a human-scaled, aesthetically pleasing environment is, possibly, still within our grasp.

Bunker Hill's Mission Apartments
The Mission Apartments (page 156) at Second and Olive Streets incorporated traditional Mission hallmarks: red clay tile roof, smooth stucco wall treatment, scalloped parapets, and wide overhanging eaves above open porches; the square bell tower evokes Mission San José. Other examples shot by Hylen include the Ems (page 158) and the Dome (page 157), the latter featuring a dome that has more in common with the "Neo-Mughal" brand of late nineteenth-century revivalist architecture than its Mission aspirations should allow.

LOS ANGELES BEFORE THE FREEWAYS

Arnold Hylen

219–227 N. Los Angeles St.
Carriage dealers Rees & Wirsching built this business block in the fall of 1883. It was designed by Charles Wellington Davis and erected by William O. Burr, and featured a cast-iron front and cast-iron cornice. To the left, the Smith & Hefner Block, also designed by Davis and built in 1883.

"In the city, time becomes visible."

— *Lewis Mumford*

a quality of loss
Affecting our Content
As Trade has suddenly encroached
Upon a sacrament

— *Emily Dickinson*

137–139 S. Broadway
Earl Bruce Millar, who made his fortune in coffee and spices, came to Los Angeles in 1880 and built one of the first grand houses on Bunker Hill, at Third and Olive Streets, in 1883. In 1886 Millar funded one of the first business blocks on Broadway, at 137–39, designed by architect William Robert Norton. It was demolished in 1958, and the block redeveloped for the California State Building.

Overleaf: Looking North at Second and Spring Streets
The seven-story Burdick Block, 127 W. Second at Spring St., is seen here under demolition in the fall of 1950. The first two stories of the Burdick Block, designed by Jasper Newton Preston, were built in 1888. In 1900, its owners added five less-ornamented floors, designed by John Parkinson. Behind it, the modernist State Division of Highways office building, completed in 1948 (and itself demolished in 2005).

THE HISTORICAL BACKGROUND 1850–1950

One of the great turning points in the history of Los Angeles began at the end of World War II, when the freeways emerged as a major civic project. An epic century as an American city had just drawn to a close and another, possibly even more spectacular, was dawning. *Life* magazine, in a special issue published June 1960, entitled: "Los Angeles: A Great City Coming of Age," reviewed the changes of this new era, and the evidence left no doubt that another historic transformation was in progress. Pressures of urban growth that had been fermenting amid the turmoil of new ideas and technologies during the war years were shaping a different city. And after the first decade of development, the freeways and all other portents of the new lifestyle, as the pages of *Life* magazine disclosed, were everywhere on the ascendant.

If Los Angeles in the 1950s was indeed a city coming of age, then the hundred years since American occupation must be regarded as one long series of dramatic steps toward maturity; perhaps the most extraordinary

A stroll on Main Street
A man walks in front of the Italian Hall (Julius Webster Krause, 1908) at 644 N. Main St. Across Macy Street to the north, the towered building at 700 North Main is the Oscar Macy block (Abram Moses Edelman, 1888). All structures on the triangle-shaped lot on which the Macy Block stood were demolished and replaced by a Standard Oil filling station in 1956; the Italian Hall remains.

in our nation's history. The spectacular transition of a little Mexican pueblo, with its huddle of sun-baked adobes, into one of the world's great cities, within so brief a span of time, still entrances the imagination. Hardly less remarkable are the more recent changes. So extensive, in fact, that to many the ante-freeway period has already begun to seem far more remote than it actually was.

Almost one hundred years before the Los Angeles issue of *Life* appeared, Theodore Hittell wrote a description that not only presents an excellent first-hand account of the local area after ten years of American administration, but a striking contrast between the rustic community of 3,500 in his day and the magnitude of the city in 1950 with its population already in excess of two million:

> The streets are mostly of good width, but they are not straight; they do not cross each other at right angles; they are not graded, nor are they paved. All the old houses are built of adobe and most of them are of one story, with flat roofs of asphaltum. The new houses are of wood and brick. On the northwestern side of town, and very near to the busy part of it, is a hill about sixty feet high, whence an excellent view of the whole place may be obtained. The vineyards and gardens are beautiful. There are about 2,500 or 3,000 acres of brilliant green—the largest body of land in vineyard, garden, and orchard within so small a space in all California. The fences fix the attention of the stranger. They are made of willow-trees, planted from nine inches to two feet apart, the spaces between the trunk being filled with poles and brush. After the fences, the stranger's notice is attracted by the *zanjas*, or irrigating ditches, which run through the town in every direction. The *zanjas* vary in size, but most of them have a body of water three feet wide, and a foot deep, running at a speed of five miles an hour…Entering the enclosures, we are among the vines, and orange, lemon, lime, citron, pear apple, peach, olive, fig and walnut trees. Some of the vines are from ten to thirty years of age. The population of the place may be described as of four equal classes, Americans, Europeans, Spanish Californians and Indians.

And he continued:

> The song of Mignon, "Knowest thou the fair land," came vividly before me as I walked through the gardens of the City of Angels. Luscious fruits, of many species and unnumbered varieties, loaded the trees. Gentle breezes came through the bowers. The waters rippled musically through the *zanjas*. Delicious odors from all the most fragrant flowers of the temperate zone permeated the atmosphere.

No doubt it was an idyllic scene, but in fact it was merely the calm before the storm. Natural catastrophes, the likes of which had never been seen, and man-made events, in their way no less unprecedented, were about to cause dramatic changes. The Dons, unaware of impending disasters, were enjoying their final days of glory, earning far greater profits from meat on the hoof than they ever had realized from hides and tallow. Never had they lived more luxuriously; never had their

Wilshire at Saint Paul Place
Rev. Asahel Morgan Hough, a Methodist Episcopal minister, came to Los Angeles in 1868. Hough established the Methodist Church in the southland, and helped found USC. He built this house at 1049 Orange St. (later Wilshire Boulevard) in mid-1893. Hough's wife, Anna Gould, was the sister of railroad tycoon Jay Gould. It eventually became a boarding house and was demolished in 1954.

ARNOLD HYLEN

women looked so glamorous. Never was their traditional largesse better served and, unhappily, the end seemed nowhere in sight.

But then came the tragic sixties with their alternating periods of devastating rainfall and withering drought, leaving most of the ranchos utterly impoverished. After the beef herds were gone, sheep-raising suddenly became profitable, and following little more than a decade of prosperity it too suffered a decline from which it never recovered. Meanwhile, the Dons had become involved in litigation with the US Land Commission, under a process of law totally alien to their own long-established codes, in an increasingly costly (and usually futile) effort to establish property rights. In the midst of all this adversity and changing times, their heritage gradually crumbled and the Arcadian interlude ended. Squatters had already blazed the way for a series of booms that were about to transform the world of the ranchos into a great American metropolis.

During the gold rush, Los Angeles prospered amid a burst of feverish activities. But during the years that followed there was a backwash of all the motley elements infesting the state, and for about twenty years lawlessness was rampant. In 1871, it reached a violent climax, when the Chinese Massacre aroused a nation-wide wave of indignation. The seventies not only brought in a return to law and order, but ushered in a number of significant events, changing the town from a rough and tumble western outpost to a modern urban community. By 1869, the Los Angeles and San Pedro Railroad had already been completed and its effects were readily apparent. The little terminal on the southwest corner of Commercial and Alameda was constantly astir with the commotion of so many new arrivals that local hotels hardly had room enough to accommodate them. Commercial Street became one of the busiest of local thoroughfares. The intersection of Los Angeles Street was the center of some of the most prominent businesses and warehouses; and scattered around the junction at Main were the Bella Union, Lafayette, and other hotels. Not to be outdone, the newly built Pico House was offering the most modern accommodations south of San Francisco.

But, exciting as they seemed, these years of lively activity were hardly more than a prelude. The influx from San Pedro was eventually to appear trivial in comparison with the overwhelming flood that would be arriving when the tracks of the Southern Pacific linking the city with San Francisco were completed September 5, 1876. It seemed incredible, barely ninety-five years after Filipe de Neve and his little band arrived, that the tide of population should have swelled to such incredible proportions. With the two new railroads, and the ease and speed of travel they provided, the total number of inhabitants increased by more than ten thousand during the early part of the seventies. But associated with the new lifestyle were the ills of its economy and, as a result, nearly one-third of this sudden growth vanished by the end of the decade, when the population had dwindled to 11,183.

Old Clay Street

338 Clay St. was one of the earlier structures on Bunker Hill. Built in 1883, its porch and frieze detailing, unadorned façade, and tall hooded windows are elements of Folk Victorian and Italianate, and characteristic of structures before Queen Anne style took hold. Clay Street, which ran from Second to Fourth between Hill and Olive Streets, was originally named Polyxena until 1883, and at only twenty feet wide, was more of an alley than a street. In the 1950s the Community Redevelopment Agency hatched plans to add sidewalk shops and cafés and make Clay a tourist destination, but ultimately opted instead to erase it from the landscape in toto.

But in 1873, while the national panic destroyed fortunes and brought financial misery to most of the country, the California economy was booming and optimism ran high. However, in August 1875 everything collapsed. Beginning with the failure of the Bank of California and the death of W.C. Ralston, banks all over the state began closing. In Los Angeles, too, there was failure and disaster. Most tragic of all was the fate of the F.P.F. Temple and Workman Bank. Faced with a shortage of funds, Temple, Workman, and their devoted friend Juan Matias Sanchez jointly mortgaged all their property to Lucky Baldwin in a futile effort to save the bank. On January 13, 1876 it was forced to close and Workman, unable to bear the shock, committed suicide. Outstanding among the few local bankers who managed to survive all this woe and travail was Isaias W. Hellman.

Eventually the West Coast proved too healthy for any prolonged aftereffects, and the eighties began on a positive note. Population and business increased steadily. Southern California, more than ever, seemed like the land of golden opportunity. Eager to capitalize on its situation to the utmost, the Southern Pacific did everything to consolidate and improve the advantages of its right-of-way. The race to develop land and trade reached a feverish pitch after November 1885, when the Santa Fe arrived. By 1887, competition had become so bitter that the now-famous rate war developed, when fares temporarily dropped to one dollar. But by then the boom of the eighties had begun to taper off, and before long there was a sudden rush to unload property. Many departed, and by the end of the decade the population, having grown to about eighty thousand in 1888, dropped to about fifty thousand.

At the close of the century, Los Angeles had reached its fiftieth anniversary as an American community. Many striking changes had taken place, but even more extraordinary things were about to happen. However, in retrospect, it is interesting to recall a variety of other events relative to these early years. Civic improvements crept along rather slowly. The first gas plant was built in 1865, just south of the Plaza Church, at the corner of Republic and New High Streets. But another decade passed before gas lamps first appeared on Main Street. A young man was hired to service them and, according to an early account, he rode horseback down the street "trailing a row of stars in the twilight." Most hotels of the period also adopted gas as a means of illumination. Six years later the first electric street lights were installed. No streets were paved until 1887, when Broadway, Spring, and Main were surfaced. In 1873, Judge R.M. Widney and John G. Downey founded the Board of Trade, and seven years later Widney and a group of friends founded the University of Southern California. The first load of oranges ever sent east was shipped by William Wolfskill in 1876, and, of course, the city enjoyed an early reputation for its vineyards and wines, some made from the San Gabriel Mission grapes.

As Los Angeles rounded out the century, the subdivision of real estate accelerated. William May Garland began developing the Westlake area in 1895, Ocean Park in 1896, Hermosa Beach in 1902, Venice in 1904, and Beverly Hills in 1907. His wife, Clara, developed Lafayette Park and presented it to the City. But even more notable, in its portent for the dawning century, was the discovery of oil by E.L. Doheny in 1892 along Glendale Boulevard, just north of Beverly. Within less than a decade, there was a swath of wells, numbering over a thousand, dotting most of the neighborhoods extending as far west as Fairfax within an area roughly spanned between the routes of Beverly and Third. By the end of the nineties, there was a sharp decline in the price of crude, and after a few years most activities had ended. But while the boom lasted, many of the home owners found themselves wealthy overnight. Emma Summers, a music teacher, became famous as "the Oil Queen"; among her investments was "The Queen," at 529 California Street, adjacent to the old Los Angeles High School, once considered the most elegant hostelry ever built on Fort Moore Hill.

During the late nineties, just as the old century was about to fade into history, there was a new addition to the horse-and-buggy traffic of Los Angeles. The automobile had arrived. It was a nemesis in the form of a gasoline engine. Few were aware how completely it was to dominate the city's future, nor that within the next fifty years nearly all the familiar sights that had so many years been their environment would vanish in its wake. Travel was about to accelerate to a degree no one would have believed, and so was the growth of the city. In 1897, the Main Street horse-carline, the last of its kind, was retired from service. At the close of the century W.A. Spalding commented that suddenly an old town had become very young, and few understood it more fully than he. During the nineties its population had more than doubled to 102,000, and within the next ten years it reached 319,000.

It would hardly be exaggerating to say that Los Angeles entered the twentieth century in high gear. It is an historical fact. By 1910, all the symptoms of the motor age were evident. Lack of regulations regarding speed, direction, and parking were already causing problems. By 1920 there were 160,000 automobiles in the city. But the leisurely pace of other days did not easily succumb. In April 1920, Mayor Snyder and the Traffic Bureau mounted a heroic effort to curb the "nuisance," only to meet with a violent outcry from local businesses, the press, and general public. The unanimous verdict was that no one wanted a "one-horse town." This attitude had already been confirmed, not only by the changes resulting from World War I, but even ten years earlier at Dominguez Field.

The Dominguez Air Meet, held January 10–20, 1910, was one of the greatest events in local as well as aviation history. Even at that early date, California had already set a long record of pioneering in the air. A major attraction of the meet was Louis Paulhan, star of the famous Rheims meet, who was paid $50,000 to participate. However, with men like Glenn Curtiss, Lincoln Beachey, and Roy Knabenshue present, America certainly did not lack talent of its own. The majority of Angelenos had never seen a plane in the sky before. They tended to regard all aviators as stuntmen and acrobats; Paulhan had, in fact, begun his career with a Parisian circus.

But Dominguez changed all that. It was the most exciting affair that had ever happened in Los Angeles. Record attendance for a single day was forty thousand. Considering that the total

population for the city was then barely 319,000, this was a remarkable turnout; enthusiasm ran so high that many businesses were obliged to give their employees time off. Several influential leaders offered substantial sums of money for a chance to fly, but all were refused. The one notable exception was William Randolph Hearst, whose flight with Paulhan created a world-wide sensation. Several exciting maneuvers were performed for the first time, and crowds gaped in breathless wonder as Paulhan made a record ascent to 4,165 feet.

The harbinger of a wonderful future had come to Los Angeles in a carnival atmosphere. In 1912 Allen and Malcolm Lougheed developed and flew their seaplane. A year later Glenn Martin and his soon-to-be-famous assistants Lawrence Bell and Donald Douglas were designing a plane that was destined to be the first ever used as a bomber. By 1920 Douglas had formed his own company. And barely twenty years later, at the outbreak of World War II, all of the local aircraft manufacturers combined were employing more people than the entire population of Los Angeles at the time of the Dominguez Meet.

Yet aircraft was only one phase of the many economic activities whose development began at the turn of the century. Equally spectacular was the growth of the entertainment industry. Around 1910, the movies and their world of make-believe arrived in force. The Hollywood dream-factories revolutionized entertainment and brought glamour, adventure, and comedy to millions. A whole pantheon of new popular idols were born overnight. During the dark days of World War I, audiences in the most remote hamlets were able to follow the struggles on the Western Front. By 1920, it was the biggest industry in Los Angeles, making about eighty percent of the world's movies. And during the twenties, it brightened up a war-weary public, and stars like Clara Bow lent a number of memorable moments to the Jazz Age. Chaplin, Pickford, and Fairbanks were honored like potentates. Their activities were followed with an almost religious fervor. The passing of few American presidents ever aroused a greater outpouring of popular sentiment than the death of Valentino.

On November 5, 1913, when Hollywood was beginning its spectacular rise, another event, hardly as glamorous, but far more vital to the future of Los Angeles, occurred at the San Fernando Mountains when water first gushed out of the Mulholland Aqueduct. Nearly thirty thousand people and a number of prominent officials were present. Many speeches were made; but the most memorable, and possibly the shortest in state history, were the words of Mulholland himself: "There it is, take it."

During the 1920s the population again doubled and for the first time rose well over a million. Los Angeles was easily the fastest growing city in the country. Several hundred tracts were put on the market and nearly 12,000 acres were subdivided. In housing alone some twenty-five thousand homes and close to a thousand new apartment houses were built. The record year for construction

Victorian Hill Street

352–58 S. Hill St. was built by Aloise Reithmuller in 1896 for the Los Angeles Fire Department; Robert Brown Young was the architect. LAFD kept it as its headquarters and as station house for Engine Company 3 until 1900. They moved across and up the street to 217 S. Hill St., at which point R.B. Young's firehouse became a commercial structure. Though it had lost its original parapet, corner towers and roof balustrade, it retained its ornamented charm. It was demolished for a parking lot in 1956.

was 1923. Prices of property doubled and tripled. Local industries reached top levels in American business. Large-scale drilling for oil began at Huntington Beach in 1920 and at Signal Hill on June 25, 1921. A new city hall, the tallest building in Los Angeles, was dedicated April 26, 1928. Other new structures were the public library and the Memorial Coliseum. In Westwood, amid rising unemployment, work was begun on UCLA.

In 1929, everything ended with a jolt, in one of the most stunning reversals ever suffered by the American economy. The thirties were almost a complete turnabout of the previous decade. Bankruptcy and loss of businesses, homes, and employment, on a scale few would have thought possible, continued year after year as if it would never end. Hollywood did its best to relieve the situation with its own brand of cinematic anodyne and a spectacular series of premiers. The year 1932 brought the Olympic Games. And during the rest of the decade, efforts were made to enliven the public gloom with a series of rousing popular events. The Elks Convention in 1936 and Armistice Day Celebration in 1938 were among the city's most ambitious. Other highlights of the decade were dedication ceremonies of the Union Station and Terminal Annex Post Office. A visit by President Franklin Delano Roosevelt topped the list.

There were many who called these years the Terrible Thirties. On the seamy side, the camera of Dorothea Lange made the classic statement in a series of scenes that rank with those of Brady as an indelible record of a national calamity. Toward the end of the decade, when the Dust Bowl began adding its misery, there were more problems. A stream of migrants, many in jalopies loaded to the top with family belongings, became a familiar sight along highways into the city, rattling along to a cacophony of pots and pans. Local citizens, already faced with more than enough problems of their own, soon took action to stem the tide. Police joined the effort. It was a tragic confrontation, but as it happened, another upheaval was brewing.

After years of a seemingly endless depression, it would have been hard to believe that this large westward movement of desperate people was in fact the vanguard of one of the greatest migrations of workers in American history. The war in Europe was causing repercussions in local aircraft plants and all related industries. And after Pearl Harbor, defense became a total effort that left very few without an occupation. Naturally there were many economic and social changes. Possibly the most historic was in the status of women. Rosie the Riveter was born, and the ancient image of women as mere homebodies was never again to be the same as great numbers took war-time jobs in business and industry. The process that began with the Pankhursts in England before World War I reached its final impetus. In science and technology there were also changes no less permanent and far-reaching. Even wartime rockets eventually served to put men on the moon and effectively probe the limits of our planetary system. And, contrary to T.S. Eliot, Hiroshima proved that the world could really end with a bang.

In Los Angeles, the changes that had been gathering momentum before Pearl Harbor revived soon after the war and continued with intensified vigor. Today, those who have little or no recollection of the city prior to 1950 hardly realize what a different place it was. Much as Los Angeles had grown before the war, it was still surrounded by great stretches of open land. Fields of alfalfa could be found only a few miles from the Civic Center. Not far beyond could be seen rolling countryside patterned with vegetable crops or row upon row of fruit trees. But after the war, and well into the 1950s, newcomers began pouring in by the thousands and everything changed.

In a city that had witnessed many migrations this was probably the biggest of all. Whole communities sprang up, practically overnight. In time pre-war Los Angeles and its outskirts were swamped in a seemingly boundless cluster of suburbs. A current jibe persisted that the suburbs were in search of a city. In fact, they were all components of a new urban configuration, a megalopolis. In the beginning, all of Los Angeles could be seen from the top of Fort Moore Hill. Today it can only be seen from an aircraft, and not even then except at a fairly high altitude. The sight is truly awesome and even somewhat frightening. By day it is a desert with rooftops, with freeways, like a network of arteries, spreading out in all directions; at dusk it becomes a carpet of light, sparkling like a galaxy of jewels.

Ever since pueblo days the pattern of growth in Los Angeles has generally been sporadic; planning, other than running streets at right angles, has usually been a matter of building wherever there was a vacant space. It became a process that kept accelerating with the years, and before the freeways no one could foresee what lay beyond the horizon. Like the city itself the freeways proliferated amid the usual political wrangling. Many mistakes were made. They were part of the city's growing pains. Planning was difficult if not impossible because the ultimate needs could not be anticipated. Yet in time all of the suburbs and outlying areas somehow became integrated by an all-embracing network of high-roads, unique in its way but, perhaps, the most logical answer to a unique situation. Los Angeles has indeed become so oriented about the automobile that the era of the freeways will forever be identified with endless traffic, parking areas, and smog, and a city of interminable concrete and asphalt instead of parks, lawns, and trees. The fate of the Plaza area and Bunker Hill will remain two of its most memorable casualties. Filipe de Neve would no doubt stagger in amazement at what has happened since his day, and we who have watched the events of this most recent transformation are almost as greatly amazed. An enlightened preservation of the past is a trust that should transcend all short-sighted considerations of the moment: it is a mark of any civilized society. If disregarded this attitude will not only leave posterity impoverished of its heritage but render the existence of all future contributions to our civic legacy equally uncertain.

Although work on the Los Angeles freeways did not become a fully organized project until after World War II, their unique origin may be said to date back to the very beginnings of the pueblo. It started along a stony and sometimes dry riverbed running southward from the San Gabriels and joined the Los Angeles River north of Elysian Park. In early days it had been

an Indian trail and later became known as Arroyo Seco. There were a number of pleasant groves along its course, and during the halcyon days of Los Angeles and Pasadena there were favorite spots for outings; one of the loveliest was Sycamore Grove.

The idea of using the Arroyo Seco as a "park-way" had been considered as far back as 1895. However, there was no definite action until about 1922, when Los Angeles, South Pasadena, and finally Pasadena began developing plans and setting aside land for that purpose. There was also the inevitable sparring between landowners, politicians, and the conservationists that was later to become one of the problems in freeway planning. Nearly eight years passed before work, spurred by the Depression and increasing joblessness, finally began moving ahead. By 1937, all of the political and financial hurdles had been cleared and at last, during the final days of 1940, the freeway was dedicated. It was not only the first in Los Angeles, but the only one in California.

After the end of World War II, there were a number of preliminaries before a peace-time economy could be geared up to prepare and proceed with the further plans. Major changes did not really become visible until the end of the decade, when extensive demolitions and excavations had become the order of the day. The long and bitter controversies that preceded all this are now practically forgotten. There was violent opposition, on both cultural and utilitarian grounds, against having

The Rochester from Court Street
The Rochester's striking façade facing Temple Street was photographed frequently (page 177), but much less so its backside. The road is North Court Street; Court split into two and formed a circle between Fremont and Beaudry, hence the curved roadway. "Court Circle" was wiped out by the Hollywood Freeway.

multiple routes of heavy traffic converge on the already congested civic center. Only a few public officials had the courage to oppose some of the ulterior motives that occasionally seemed to conflict with public interest; notable among these was John Anson Ford. The many problems in urban planning that marked this transitional period are effectively summarized in an article entitled "The Los Angeles Experience" by Martin J. Schiesel in the Summer 1980 issue of *California History*.

But now that the scene has changed, there is no choice other than to take a philosophical glance at recent events and hope that the future will not be quite so devastating. On July 9, 1980, when the old Bixby home in Long Beach was being demolished, one of the news reporters observed: "Our bicentennial is just around the corner but we will soon need a surveyor to tell us where most of our landmarks once stood." During the bicentennial Los Angeles can certainly take pride in the numerous triumphs of two hundred incredible years, even though many of its most famous landmarks have become a gallery of ghosts, fortunately rescued from oblivion through the continued devotion of local artists and historians.

In the summer of 1872 Waite & Beane, job printers at 14 Commercial St., published the first *Los Angeles Directory*. The city was still a very small place then, with a population somewhere around six thousand. Street numbers began at the Plaza and ended in the vicinity of Fourth Street. After that the houses were few and far between, and locations were described as being "beyond" Fifth, or Sixth, and so on. There were no streets identified as north, east, south, or west. Commenting on the directory, some years later, J.M. Guinn remarked that a telescope might have served the purpose just as well.

Most of the city could be seen from Poundcake Hill at the southeast corner of Temple and Broadway. Better still was the view from the hills along the western perimeter of the city. The classic vantage point was a location a short distance north of Fort Moore, overlooking the Plaza area. It was from there that both W.R. Hutton and Charles Koppel sketched their well-known panoramas around the 1850s. The view here, reproduced from almost the same vantage point, shows how it has changed in one hundred years.

During the intervening century the long slope ending a short distance from the Plaza Church has undergone several changes in contour. Of these, two in particular made lasting differences in the appearance of the hill. The first was in 1932 when the route of Spring Street, which originally veered northeast beyond First, was straightened to run due north. As a result, the east slope of Fort Moore Hill was partially cut away between Temple and Sunset, leaving a steep bluff along the west side of Spring for many years. The second change occurred when the bluff, and North Broadway Tunnel underneath, were excavated to make room for the freeway. This area, freshly leveled off, is visible in the foreground of the photograph. The steps on the left once afforded access from Sunset to the old Los Angeles High School and the extensive neighborhood that formerly occupied the hill.

Plaza Area from Fort Moore Hill
A man walks from Fort Moore Hill toward the corner of Sunset and Broadway. From the steps, he approaches 400 Sunset Blvd., a brick commercial building built in 1922 with "Barber Shop" painted on the back. It survived until 2016, when it was demolished for a 355-unit residential project. Structures that still survive are visible in the distance, e.g., the Plaza Church and the towers of United Methodist Church and Union Station, but the vast majority of this landscape has been erased and its streets realigned.

Extending diagonally toward the Plaza is Sunset Boulevard, formerly called Short and/or Marchessault. The entire area north of Sunset (left of view) and as far east as Main was once the site of Sonoratown and, still earlier, the location of the original pueblo founded by Felipe de Neve in 1781. It is generally assumed that the southeast corner of the early pueblo and the northwest corner of the current Plaza joined somewhere in the vicinity of Sunset and Main. The first church, or chapel, and the *cuartel* stood approximately in the center of the picture, where the filling station is located.

The site of the present church was chosen after a period of trial and error. The shops and administrative offices that once surrounded the north side of the church formed a patio that was for years one of its most pleasant features. A gnarled trunk of an old vine twisted upward in the center. Its tendrils spread a canopy between the buildings, filtering the sunlight into pleasant leaf-green shade. The patio was often the lively scene of wedding parties and anniversaries as well as bazaars and numerous seasonal festivities. The old tradition of colorful costumes and bright displays of garlands and lanterns, so typical of old California celebrations, religious and secular alike, continued as long as the patio remained.

At the north end of Olvera Street, near the foot of an olive tree planted by Christine Sterling, there is an old stone trough. While it is sometimes thought to have been used for watering horses, more recent opinion seems to agree that it is a *molcajéte* once used by the Gabrielino Indians★. And since they were the original inhabitants of the Los Angeles area, and remnants of their existence are few, it seems fitting that they should be commemorated by this typical relic of their culture.

According to Mrs. Sterling, it was discovered by R.W. Hamsher under an old olive tree while he was investigating sources of local history. On January 10, 1930, she noted in her diary that the department of water and power had "made the most wonderful gift to the street," and that in memory of the place where it was first found she had "lovingly" placed it beneath a similar tree on Olvera Street.

Patio of Plaza Church

The graceful arcade seen surrounding the patio had been built as part of the rear façade of Citizens Trust & Savings Bank (Gene Verge Sr., 1924). The archdiocese demolished the bank in 1972, and constructed a smaller version of the arcaded structure, designed by the firm of O'Leary & Terasawa, which also designed a new rectory at the northwest corner of the property.

This type of *metáte*, or mortar, is said to have been almost exclusively typical among the Indians of Southern California. Much of the food they consumed consisted of a variety of nuts and seeds ground by means of a *mano*, or pestle, usually cylindrical, with rounded ends and about three inches in diameter. Acorns, because of their abundance, were one of the principal foods. After being ground they were thoroughly leached in hot water until all bitterness was gone, and the resulting dough was used in much the same manner as the masa that Mexicans made from corn.

Olvera Street, as it looks today, is a monument to Christine Sterling. Were it not for her love, foresight, and dogged persistence, relics like the Avila Adobe, and Pelaconi House, would have been swept away, and the little thoroughfare she struggled so valiantly to preserve would never have survived. All that existed when she began was a broad unkempt lane, strewn with rubbish, and a few vermin-ridden buildings on either side crumbling in decay. It had already been marked for demolition, and the Plaza itself was being considered for the site of a new railroad station. An attempt to avert all this posed a formidable task for a lone woman with infinitely more courage than resources. But help eventually came in the form of Harry Chandler and several other public-spirited citizens.

Originally, as W. W. Robinson so aptly remarked, Olvera was "a very short street." The name, derived from Don Augustin Olvera, whose adobe once faced the Plaza just east of the street, is of recent date. Once it was known as Wine Street, a cul-de-sac formed by a wing of the Avila Adobe and the Casa Seguro, a bar and gambling casino from which it may originally have gotten the name. A narrow passageway between the two buildings led to the Zanja Madre. At this point it was a waterway several feet wide, running southeasterly from the intersection of Main and Macy across a field at the rear of the Sepúlveda, Avila, and Olvera properties.

Among various entries in her diary for February 1930, Mrs. Sterling notes that a fountain was

*Gabrielino Metáte (mortar)

Landscape contractor Robert W. Hamsher unearthed this *metáte* from beneath an olive tree near the Chatsworth Reservoir in 1930, on land owned by the Los Angeles Bureau of Power and Light. The bureau then gifted the object to Christine Sterling's Olvera Street restoration project; for decades, Canoga Park officials pressed downtown civic leaders in charge of Olvera Street to have the prized artifact returned to its original location. It was later discovered to *not* be an artifact of early Indigenous people; rather, rancher August Schweikhard had hand-carved the sandstone "relic" as an animal watering trough in 1897. The trough has now been bricked in, and the olive tree replaced by a ficus.

being built in connection with a diagonal course of bricks marking the place where the Zanja Madre once crossed Olvera Street. Other items indicate that the Sepúlveda Block had been leased from Mrs. Gibbs on February 15, and, that on the 25th, Mrs. Florence Walker was already busily at work carving the large cross that now stands at the entrance on Sunset. She also expressed a particular wish that the street should always be known as El Paseo de Los Angeles.

After the Avila Adobe had been restored, she borrowed authentic furnishings from Rancho Palos Verdes, the home of Señora Rudecinda Sepúlveda, in order to recreate as much of the original atmosphere as possible. In the parlor there was even a large framed photograph of Señora Encarnación Avila on the wall flanked by two smaller ones of Pio and Andrés Pico. Here also she placed an image of the Virgin of Guadalupe "and kept a candle burning night and day." And only when the elderly *Californios* came to visit, exclaiming that it seemed to bring back the past, did she at last feel satisfied.

The Avila Adobe dates from about 1818. It is the oldest residence in Los Angeles and was originally almost twice the present size. In happier days it was one of the community's liveliest centers of hospitality. But after the death of Don Francisco in defense of the pueblo and the arrival of Stockton in January 1847, the pleasant times ended. The sudden flight of Encarnación appeared to symbolize all that happened; the climax of an idyllic way of life.

In general, the appearance of early Los Angeles was very similar to many old pueblos still to be seen in parts of the Southwest. The adobes were so well adapted to their setting that they seemed almost indigenous. But, humble as they were, they sheltered a people whose vivacity and gracious mode of existence lent a special charm to *Californio* ways. On departing from Los Angeles in 1848, one young American officer wrote that he felt sad at heart, not so much for leaving the "poor pile of adobes" as for the kind hearts and endearing souls who dwelt within. Today the Avila Adobe seems to have lost some of the charm that Christine Sterling had recaptured. Excepting the church, it is the only early adobe left standing near the Plaza.

Interior of Avila Adobe: Olvera Street

Hylen's photographs inside the Avila Adobe provide a record of Sterling's renovation of the interior into an approximation of a Mexican-era residence. After the 1971 earthquake, the interior was heavily remodeled, based on archaeological investigations; it was subsequently remodeled again, and returned to its pre-Mexican roots as a Spanish structure.

Two others, formerly located nearby, were casualties of redevelopment.

One of these, the Casa Lugo, was the last of the notable adobes that once faced directly on the Plaza. It stood on the east side of Los Angeles Street and was originally the home of Don Vicente Lugo. It was the only two-story adobe in that area and considerably altered since the late 1830s when it was first built. The Lugos were one of the most influential early families. Vicente's brother, Don José del Carmen Lugo, was very active in local affairs and served as the first *alcalde* under the American flag. About 1867, Vicente Lugo donated the building to Saint Vincent's College, which after years of steady growth was eventually to become Loyola University. In the beginning it provided elementary as well as high school and college classes. Many of the community's most prominent citizens were among its earliest students. But the school soon outgrew its space and moved to the south side of Sixth Street between Hill and Broadway. And in the course of time the adobe became a part of Chinatown and the red-light district, housing a variety of shady operations, including fan-tan and opium, for several years.

The other, known as the Talamentes Adobe, stood on the west side of Broadway, flush against the rear wall of the old Bozzani Garage at the corner of Sunset. It was the last remnant of Sonoratown. In recent years the surface of Broadway had been raised so much that the level of the adobe (page 17) was almost a couple of feet below that of the sidewalk; so that huddled behind the garage and partly hidden by a signboard, it ended its days practically unnoticed.

There is little information about the adobe. Among the few facts known with reasonable certainty is that it originally belonged to Tómas Talamentes, a nephew of José María Avila, and later became the property of José Mascarel. Mascarel is said to have been a sea captain who came to Los Angeles in 1844. He married an Indian woman and soon established a very prosperous business in Sonoratown. Eventually he made many important investments in local property, including the famous Mascarel Ranch, later to become world-renowned as Hollywood. In 1865, he became mayor of Los Angeles. During this period he was also involved in several transactions

Patio of Avila Adobe: Olvera Street
It is difficult to comprehend that such an important and intact structure as the Avila Adobe was scheduled for demolition, but such was Los Angeles in the 1920s. Christine Sterling was exceptionally lucky to raise funds for its purchase and restoration immediately before the Depression hit. She lived in the adobe until her death in 1963.

along Commercial Street, at which time the Broadway adobe was sold to a jeweler named Santa Cruz for additional funds.

Through most of the sixties, the Plaza retained much of its old pueblo atmosphere. Nearly all of the early adobes still remained intact: the Avila and Olvera on the north side; the Casa Lugo on the east; and, on the south, the Coronel, Sepúlveda, and Carrillo adobes. The Coronel and Carrillo adobes, in particular, were centers of some of the most lavish and brilliant affairs of their time. But in 1870, when Pío Pico decided to build his soon-to-be-famous hotel, the Carrillo homestead with its pleasant memories was doomed. So was the old-fashioned pueblo atmosphere of the Plaza, and a series of changes began that finally erased most vestiges of its earlier days.

The lone survivor of all these historic places is the little church on the west side of the Plaza, Nuesta Señora La Reina de Los Angeles. After many hazards and changes it continues to symbolize the heritage and character of the city to a degree that is the very essence of Los Angeles. Yet when the *Times* asked ten leading authorities to name twelve of the "most significant" landmarks in Los Angeles, not one named the Plaza Church. During the course of its history, La Reina has undergone several transformations, inside and out, but its Franciscan simplicity is still

Casa Lugo: Los Angeles Street near Sunset
The move to demolish the Lugo Adobe began in 1934, when plans for Union Station called for the area to its west to be redeveloped as parkland. Despite a 1939 designation of Casa Lugo as California Historical Landmark No. 301, landmark status could not prevent its demolition in February 1951. The subsequent park on the site was named for Father Junipero Serra. At center, the Romanesque-style Breed Block (1899; Robert Brown Young, attributed).

Talamentes Adobe: Broadway near Sunset
This adobe stood at 639–643 N. Broadway; it was demolished in 1957, and the site remained a parking lot until 2012. The Bozzani Motors building was built as a Los Angeles & Redondo Railway Depot, and was demolished for a surface lot in 1963.

Veranda of Talamentes Adobe

Built in 1835, the Talamentes Adobe was Los Angeles's second-oldest dwelling. Through 1956, the Native Sons of the Golden West were in negotiations with owner Alfred Chapman to purchase the house and restore it, but it was nevertheless demolished for reasons unknown.

Overleaf: Intersection of Sunset and Main, looking northwest

The Hotel Pacific, designed by Dennis & Farwell and built in 1910, was demolished for parking lots in 1957, along with the other buildings visible to the north of the Plaza church.

perceptible and the River of Life doors continue to exemplify the basic verities that the founders of our state and community held in greatest veneration.

Sometime in 1814, Fra Luis Gil y Taboada, recently arrived at San Gabriel, addressed a petition to Fra José Señan proposing a church in Los Angeles. The request was granted, but it remained for Fra Mariano Payeras to make it a reality. It was his untiring energy and devotion, and his alone, that ultimately saw the project to completion. The dedication did not take place until nearly eight years later, on December 8, 1822. The interim had been a seemingly endless period of begging, cajoling, and coaxing by Payeras. The church is a monument to Payeras.

For the next half-century or more the little church was the center of life in Los Angeles. A number of years passed before there was any other place of worship, so it was not uncommon to find Protestants in the congregation. Morning, noon, and night the bells of the *campanario* were sounded and the devout *pobladores* humbly knelt in prayer wherever they happened to be. Judge Hayes recalled how the kneeling congregation on Sundays and high holy-days looked like a flower garden in full bloom. At one time there was a cemetery at the south side of the church and, on the north, the rectory with a long verandah facing a garden surrounded by a picket fence. But, as

Nuestra Señora La Reina de Los Angeles
The church was completely rebuilt in 1861, after its façade collapsed onto the street following heavy rains in 1859. Another rebuild in 1912 restored the three-bell *campanario* which had been removed in the 1861 remodel. Known as "La Placita," it is the only building at El Pueblo that maintains its original purpose.

the city continued to grow, the cemetery became a parking lot and the rectory, after having been transformed into a patio for many years, was eliminated to meet the need for expansion.

During the first decades of its existence many of the old Mexican folkways related to the church continued to be observed. Between the celebrations of holy days, and numerous fiestas, the entire year was almost a continuous round of festivities. The *Californios* had a distinct native flair for imbuing even the simplest ritual with an extra dimension of color and gayety, most of which gradually vanished as the more austere Yankee ethic began to predominate.

Some of the most exciting occasions were *Pascuas*, or Easter, with the lively punishment of Judas on Good Friday; Corpus Christi, and its feasting, dancing and *Correr el Gallo*; and culminating the year's festivities, *La Navidad*, with its *Los Pastores* and the solemn but colorful candle-lit procession of

Left: Interior of Plaza Church (1950)
Contemporary visitors to the Plaza Church will note its interior has undergone major changes since Hylen's photograph. The western end of the 1818 church was demolished by the diocese in 1965 in order to build an adjacent church facing Spring Street, designed by architect Damon Edward Spitzer. Moreover, the skylight seen in Hylen's image was filled in, and the walls whitewashed.

Right: Dia de la Reina, Plaza Church, August 15, 1950
Most elements of the sanctuary, including the altar and the statue of the Virgin, were lost when the church demolished the apse, although some of the art remains. For example, the painting *Saint Francis Receiving the Stigmata* (a decent copy of Frans Pourbus the Younger's 1620 oil) seen to the right of the statue of Mary was worked into the new altar.

Las Posadas at Christmas time followed by the nightly breaking of piñatas amid cries of delight from children and grown-ups alike. These were some of the most popular holidays. But one of the most ancient and popular of all, and celebrated with great enthusiasm as long as the *Californios* reigned, slowly vanished and is now scarcely remembered; it was St. John's Day.

However, the pueblo had a holiday uniquely its own, the Dia de Nuestra Senõra La Reina de Los Angeles. This has always been one of the Catholic high holy-days, but it was formerly observed with a degree of public fervor and participation no longer a part of the local scene. During the California Centennial, memories of this custom seemed to come alive once more in the image of the Virgin that brightened the altar of La Reina. An article that appeared in the *The Star* on August 22, 1857, recaptures the essence of its meaning and the spirit of a time when the community was far smaller and much more closely knit:

> …the 15th of August is celebrated as the anniversary of the patron saint of our vineyard city…After the conclusion of early mass, and at about 9 o'clock a.m., high mass was celebrated in the Catholic Church…At the conclusion of the mass, the pupils of the female school, headed by the instructresses, the Sisters of Charity, came out of the church in procession, bearing the image of our Lady under a canopy; they were joined by the Lancers, and passing around the public square, re-entered the church. The appearance of the procession as it left the church, and during its march, was imposing. The canopy covering the representation of the angelic queen, tastefully ornamented, was borne by girls dressed in white. The girls of the school, with their heads uncovered, and in uniform white dresses, followed; then came the Lancers, the rear of the company being brought up by a mounted division, which (armed with lances) had been on duty during the morning…A bull-fight took place in the upper part of town, in the afternoon, which was attended by a dense crowd of spectators. This diversion, as usual, was attended with various casualties.

In view of the bicentennial, now in progress, it is interesting to recall events one hundred years ago and how it was observed by the Plaza Church. Since then, Los Angeles has become largely isolated from its past. As Michael Caine commented, this is "the most shifting, impermanent city on earth." Small wonder, then, that the present celebration has overlooked so many of its early beginnings. In 1881 the Plaza with its little church and cluster of historic places was unanimously regarded as all that was most representative of the city's origins.

As part of the celebration Father Verdaguer had a platform erected facing the Plaza just south of the church. It was decorated with large portraits of President Garfield, the Pope, and King Alphonso draped with garlands of evergreen. On the evening of September 4, before an audience that crowded the Plaza from the platform to "Mrs. Jones's building on the east to the lower edge on the west," the front of the church was brightly illuminated by gaslight at the stroke of seven o'clock. Judge Sepúlveda reviewed events of the first hundred years, and Don Juan Toro spoke

Overleaf: Main Street, looking northwest from Commercial
This strip was demolished in early 1957. It is now the site of the Los Angeles Mall and Fletcher Bowron Square, built in 1974 and dedicated in 1975.

a few words in Spanish to the numerous Latinos who were present. Father Verdaguer ended the speeches with a prayer for the recovery of President Garfield who was dying from the wound of an assassin's bullet. The ceremonies closed with a song recital by fifty girls from the sister's school "accompanied by Miss Sacriste at the piano."

By the end of the sixties the pastoral era and the time-honored old customs of the Dons had already begun to seem quaint and out of phase with the time. Like Pío Pico and others, Abel Stearns foresaw the growing need to adapt his thinking to the newer ideas. Accordingly, in 1857 he built the first modern commercial building in Los Angeles, the Arcadia Block, using "one million one hundred fifty thousand bricks," to repel the dangers of fire and flood. It stood on the west side of Los Angeles Street at the corner of Arcadia, back to back with the famous old Palacio. And when the devastating floods of the sixties brought wrack and ruin to so many old adobes, the Stearns Block remained undamaged, proving the need of more advanced construction methods.

As the city continued to grow, most of the finer buildings were erected along Main and Spring Streets. According to J.A. Graves, the highest priced real estate in 1875 was on both sides of Main from the St. Charles Hotel (Commercial Street) to the Temple Block. Many of the finest residences during that period were located along Main and Spring, south of Second, terminating with the spacious Downey, Workman, and Orzo Childs estates beyond Ninth Street. For several miles to the east of this area were the orchards and vineyards of Wolfskill, Kohler, Frohling, and Weil.

By 1950, when work on the freeways was gathering momentum, very few of the old buildings were left on Main north of First. Most of them had been demolished during the twenties, when the early central business district of Los Angeles, a triangular section of blocks bounded by First, Main, and old Spring Streets, was cleared away to make room for the new city hall. However, nearly everything on the east side of Main escaped destruction several decades longer. But during that interim a few of the most famous of these remaining landmarks were destroyed.

Among the buildings that continued to survive the most noteworthy were located along the "historic mile" between the Plaza and Commercial Street. Here even the yawning gaps left by the Bella Union and the Baker Block (which stood on ground once occupied by the Stearns Palacio) arrested the eye; mute reminders of the past and impending changes (page 187). Excepting the Plaza, few places had witnessed so many exciting episodes in the early history of Los Angeles. How often this area appears in the background of old photographs. The men and activities associated with it figured in some of the most exciting events of the time.

Most familiar of these landmarks were Pico's Building and the Bella Union. Few who passed the vacant site suspect how much history had transpired there. Indian graves were found when the site was first cleared. The original adobe served briefly as the state capitol during Pío Pico's governorship and later became Gillespie's headquarters during his short-lived term as administrator of the pueblo during the American occupation in 1846. Eventually it became the location of the first hotel in Los Angeles, the Bella Union; an amazing chapter of local history in itself.

It was for many years a center of the community's most important social and political events. Notables, such as Generals Sherman and John C. Frémont, were among the many celebrities who were honored with banquets and addressed crowds from its balcony. The hotel took pride in its cuisine as the best in Los Angeles. The Isaias Hellmans celebrated their wedding there, as did Isaac Van Nuys and Susanna Lankershim and a number of other prominent citizens. A few Angelenos made the hotel their home, and C.A. Ducommun was born there. It was also the locale of the Carlisle-King shoot-out, one of the most spectacular gunfights in the annals of the West. On November 26, 1877, the first words ever spoken over a telephone in Los Angeles were heard in conversation between the Bella Union and the Lafayette Hotel on the opposite side of Main Street. The protests of environmentalists were also heard when three fine locust trees that had graced the front of the hotel for years were cut down. One of the last events of any consequence was in December 1882 when a 150-foot pole, holding aloft one of the seven first electric street-lamps ever used in Los Angeles, was erected in front of the hotel.

The little two-story building adjacent to the lot where the hotel once stood was the humble birthplace of one of the city's largest financial institutions, the Security First National Bank. Designed by Ezra F. Kysor, it was originally built by Pío Pico as an investment. Their initial occupant was

Downey Block, Grand Central Hotel, and Pico's Building
Grand Central Hotel was also known as the Perry & Riley Block. Its original incarnation (before a December 1875 transformation) was as Backman House, a hotel under the proprietorship of a Mrs. Backman, who opened the establishment in November 1874.

Hellman, Temple & Co., a partnership formed by William Workman and Francis Pliny Fiske Temple, with Isaias W. Hellman as manager; the first formal bank in Los Angeles. It opened September 1, 1868. Early in 1871, Hellman bought out his partners and continued the bank as I.W. Hellman & Co. But shortly thereafter Hellman, together with a group of local business men, including Childs, Ducommun, and Amestoy formed the Farmers & Merchants Bank of Los Angeles. Only the name Bank of Los Angeles appears on the triangular capstone seen in the early photographs because the first two words in the name were accidentally omitted.

By the summer of 1874, the bank had found its quarters on the first floor of the Pico building too small and moved across Main in the Wollweber building adjoining the south side of the Lafayette Hotel. Ten years later the bank moved its quarters to the southeast corner of Main and Commercial, where it remained for the next twenty years. Finally, in 1905, the bank moved into a massive new neoclassical building on the southwest corner of Fourth and Main. It was a choice location then, with two of the city's most elegant hotels as neighbors: the Van Nuys on the northwest corner, and on the northeast, its popular rival, the Westminster. On September 28, 1956, with resources of $355,876,000 it merged with the Security-First National Bank, whose total holdings at that time amounted to $2,189,948,000.

On the second floor of the Pico building was another tenant whose achievements were equally notable; Judge Robert M. Widney, one of the founders of the University of Southern California. Among numerous other achievements, he took an active part in organizing the Main Street Railway. It ran south on Main from the Plaza to First, and then to the Bellevue Terrace Hotel on the northwest corner of Sixth and Figueroa, by way of Spring Street. He was also instrumental in the founding of Long Beach and one of the first promoters of local real estate on a nation-wide scale.

In 1880 Pío Pico, more involved than ever in the trammels of a legal process he never really understood, lost both the building and his hotel when a firm of San Francisco investors foreclosed on his properties.

Adjoining the northern side of Pico's building was the Grand Central Hotel. In 1874, a party of entrepreneurs, William Perry and James Riley, entered into an agreement with Pico allowing them to use the north wall of his property as part of the three-story building they proposed to erect. Newspaper ads of that period described the Grand Central as "a family hotel." A few years after it was built, it was acquired as an annex by the Bella Union and a passage was cut through Pico's Building, connecting the two hotels.

At the northern side of the Grand Central was a small building whose slender proportions

Den's Building

This building was developed by Governor John G. Downey and was known as the Downey Block (Charles Wellington Davis, 1878). The term "block" was once standard in referring to an office building, e.g., the Downey Block or the Bradbury Block, which were office blocks named for their builders.

Overleaf: Ducommun Block

The Ducommun Block, right, was built in 1874; the architect was Ezra Kysor. The structure to its north, with the double-height, cornice-topped square bays, dates to about 1885. These structures were demolished by Security First National Bank in mid-1951, and replaced by a modernist bank building designed by Austin, Field & Fry.

and elegant style contrasted sharply with its neighbors. Standing as if crushed between the Grand Central on one side and the massive Baker Block that once stood on the other, its unique charm compensated for whatever it lacked in size. Architecturally it was one of the most graceful of its contemporaries. Its refinement naturally reflected the taste of its owner; one of the most colorful and sophisticated citizens of early Los Angeles, Doctor Richard Somerset Den. The entire façade was carved of white marble and imported from Italy. Even when it was first completed, those who knew him recognized the doctor's character in every line. He was a man of distinction, and this was exactly the sort of building they would have expected of him.

Dr. Den himself always cut a dashing figure in public. He was an avid fancier of horses and always appeared on a high-stepping jet-black mount. The doctor was usually seen riding in a dark Prince Albert coat, sometimes with a velvet collar, wearing a top-hat and high stock collar with a trim black tie. In an age of side-burns, beards, and goatees, he remained clean-shaven, revealing a florid complexion and wisps of white hair curling up under the brim of his hat.

Richard Den was the first professionally trained doctor to settle in Los Angeles. On arrival from Dublin he spent some time

Pico House, Theater Mercedes, and Masonic Hall
*About the Masonic Hall, Hylen is incorrect (page 80): the Main Street lodge rooms for Los Angeles No. 42 (chartered 1854), were built in 1858; the architects were lumberman William Hayes Perry and his partner James Brady, although the building was finished by Perry and new partner Wallace Woodworth. Hylen's assertion in *Before the Freeways* in fact refers to Lodge 42's *second* home, the Weston-designed lodge building at 153 N. Spring St., where the group met from 1868–1896.

with an elder brother who had settled in Santa Barbara and, attracted by the life-style and opportunities in Southern California, decided to stay. As a typical Irishman the love of horseflesh was in his blood, and in this he found plenty of good company among the *Californios*. Before long he was on friendly terms with most of the leading Dons. During the struggle between the Yankees and the Mexicans he treated the wounded of both armies with equal care at an improvised hospital furnished by Don Luis Vignes. During the years that followed, his ties with Santa Barbara grew closer and he acquired half interest in the family ranch at San Marcos. But the remainder of his life was spent in Los Angeles, saddened by many losses in his family. Pioneers like Newmark, Workman, and Graves remembered him with affection.

The only other contemporary building to survive in this vicinity was the Ducommun Block, on the northeast corner of Main and Commercial, formerly one of the city's busiest intersections. Charles Louis Ducommun arrived in Los Angeles during the gold rush and opened a watchmaker's shop just south of the Bella Union. Since gold dust was being used as a medium of exchange he soon became active in various transactions involving cash value and expanded stock to include jewelry, cutlery, hardware, and an extensive line of other practical items. By 1854, his business had done so well that he was able to buy the corner where his building, another of Kysor's designs, was to be erected some nineteen years later. In 1865 he became one of the organizers of the Los Angeles Pioneer Oil Company, Inc., the first in California. He was also a founding member of the Farmers and Merchants Bank, as well as the Main & Agricultural Park Railway.

Still standing, at the northern end of the "historic mile" are the Pico House, Teatro Mercedes, and the Masonic Hall. Continuing southward, the wide gap created by the freeway and its off-ramp to Los Angeles Street at Aliso, was for several decades the site of Abel Stearns Palacio and the Arcadia Block, both razed in the 1870s to make way for the Baker Block, also demolished some sixty years later. And now that these and every other landmark on the east side of Main Street as far as First are gone, only the little cluster adjoining the Plaza remains.

Fortunately they have all been carefully restored, but not altogether in the manner that Christine Sterling tried to achieve. Everything is neat and tidy, but the former ambience is gone. No doubt many will be happy enough, perhaps even thankful, for the absence of the former atmosphere: the piquant mélange of Latin sounds and odors, the lively chatter, the mariachi juke boxes, and the tangy aromas of Mexican food that pervaded the area when this view was taken.

The cornerstone of the Pico House was laid September 18, 1869 on the former site of the Carrillo adobe, one of the most notable landmarks of the early pueblo. The building was designed by Kysor and completed in June 1870 at a cost of $85,000. The furnishings were estimated to have cost an additional $34,000. On the first floor there were shops along Main Street, three dining rooms facing the Plaza, and a porte cochère, offices, and kitchen facing Sanchez. In the center of the building was a patio and fountain. A fine stairway led to elegantly furnished rooms for social events, cards, and billiards. There were also a number of suites, all tastefully decorated, as were the

Sepúlveda Block
Corterisan & Merithew designed the Sepúlveda Block, completed in the fall of 1887. The robust massing of the exaggerated square bays, counterbalanced with the lacy decorative cresting, lend this structure a particularly Eastlake feel.

bedrooms on the third floor. It was inaugurated with a splendid flourish. Local society attended in force, with Doña Luisa Garfias, daughter of José María and Encarnación Avila, clasping the arm of Pío Pico at the head of the procession. Many celebrities stopped there, including Archduke Ludwig Salvator, who remained incognito while writing *Los Angeles in the Sunny Seventies: A Flower from the Golden Land*; Helen Hunt Jackson, while gathering material for *Ramona*, and Colonel and Arcadia Stearns de Baker, while the Baker Block was under construction.

Teatro Merced, adjoining the Pico House, was built on a lot once occupied by the Eldorado Bar which, together with the Casa Lugo and the Bell Block, was among the only two-story buildings then located in the vicinity of the Plaza. It also had the further distinction of being the first prefabricated frame building ever erected in Los Angeles, having been cut and shipped from around the Horn from Boston. It was later purchased by Reverend Adam Bland, stripped of its "sacrilegious trappings," and converted into a Methodist church. When William Abbot and his wife Doña Merced Garcia bought the property, the wooden building was moved by its new owner to a location somewhere on nearby Aliso Street.

When Abbot suggested the idea of constructing a three-story edifice with stores at street-level, a theater on the second floor, and living-quarters on the third, Doña Merced is reported to have agreed on condition that it would be taller than the Pico House. After all, most of the money belonged to her. Ezra F. Kysor, architect of the Pico House, was chosen to handle the work, late in July 1870, barely a month after the hotel was completed. Kysor was evidently a resourceful designer, because he not only increased the height but used a few optical devices that helped to provide an even greater illusion of size. The height of the second floor was increased to almost twenty-five percent above that of the hotel and the windows made almost twice as large. These features raised the total height well above the roof level of the Pico House so that, including the pediment with its arched centerpiece, the façade in effect appeared ten or twelve feet higher than that of the hotel. A more generous spacing between the window of the upper stories, plus the bulky appearance of the ornamental balcony that formerly spanned the sidewalk, further enhanced the size. The whole concept was a rather fascinating architectural tour de force that local historians somehow appear to have overlooked.

Contrary to the popular notion, it was not the first theater in Los Angeles. During its existence there were many ups and downs. Not many companies ventured so far south in those days, and after its opening night on Friday, December 30, 1870, when the Wilmington 21st Regiment Band and some local artists gave a concert, scheduled entertainments were never fulfilled. The only break was a demonstration of laughing-gas, when members of the audience volunteered and enjoyed a side-splitting evening watching each other's antics. On January 30, 1871, performances were resumed with a presentation of *Fanchon*, starring Miss Kitty Blanchard, before a very fashionable audience and repeated the following night with great success. Then followed the first local performance ever of a male impersonation when Miss Blanchard appeared before a goggle-

Sentous Block
The Sentous Block was designed by Burgess J. Reeve and built in the spring of 1886. Former governor Pío Pico, having lost his fortune to gambling, overspending, and property disputes, spent his declining years in an apartment at the Sentous. Just before its August 1957 demolition, Christine "The Mother of Olvera Street" Sterling hung a black wreath on its door.

eyed audience as the Earl of Darnley in *Field of Cloth and Gold*. As time passed, shows ran the gamut from Shakespeare to slapstick. There were popular melodramas, minstrels, and Mexican music with dancing, and one of two high-school graduations for good measure. In 1876, after an interval during which it was used as Armory for the Los Angeles Guards, Abbot's widow renewed her efforts to revive the theater, only to fail again. Meanwhile audiences were being lured away by Childs's opera house and other new places of entertainment.

Oldest of the three buildings is the Masonic Hall, dedicated Thursday, December 29, 1868★. The news report dated January 1, 1869 provides an intimate picture of the occasion, and the hall as it originally appeared, in rhetoric typical of the period:

> …at three o'clock P.M.…a large number of members of the sister lodges and ladies and gentlemen of the city were present. At the close of the ceremonies, the Acting Grand Master, S. Prager, made a few appropriate remarks, and was followed by Rev. A.W. Edelman, who delivered an able and absolutely dedicatory address, after which there was music by the choir, and Hon. C.E. Thom, orator of the day, was introduced, and delivered an address that for historic truth and elegance deserves the first place in the gems of Masonic literature…At half past eight o'clock, P.M., the members of the fraternity and a number of invited guests partook of a splendid collation at the Lafayette Hotel, at which the most happy feeling prevailed. The hall itself is an imposing building, two stories high, and thirty-five by eighty feet deep, and erected under the supervision of E.J. Weston, Architect. The lodge rooms are well ventilated, and furnished throughout in the most elegant manner, handsome carpets on the floor, and all the usual furniture of a lodge-room of the finest quality; is lighted by three elegant chandeliers and a number of jets, making twenty-five lights in all, and is a credit to the taste and liberality of the officers and members of the Los Angeles Lodge.

North of the Plaza, between Sunset and Macy, along a section of Main formerly known as Bath Street, there were several buildings dating back to the Victorian period. Today only two remain, both on the east side of the street. One is the Pelanconi Block, built in 1850 by an Austro-Italian named Guiseppe Covacichi and sold in 1865 to Antonio Pelanconi, an Italian vintner. It was one of the first brick buildings ever erected in Los Angeles, and originally intended to be a combination of residence and wine cellar. The other is the Sepúlveda Block, dating from 1888 and built by Eloisa Martínez de Sepúlveda as a residence and hotel. Directly across the street, at 615–619 North Main, the Sentous Block languished for several years before it was demolished. Like many of the other old buildings, its history was long forgotten. Even the name, once familiar, had become an enigma to the average passerby. Like Amestoy, Louis Sentous was another immigrant whose life was an extraordinary success story. In fact, their lives were remarkably parallel. Both arrived in California almost penniless; both began their careers in the gold fields and both became ranchers; the only exception being that Sentous chose to deal in cattle rather than sheep. And this

Los Angeles Street, looking south from the Plaza
The tattered awning once advertised Jerry's Joynt, home of the famous Jade Lounge. It was demolished in 1951. The spot where the man stands is now an on-ramp to the 101 freeway.

in itself was rather unusual because, even though the times were generally regarded as disastrous for the local cattle business, he continued to make very lucrative deals. Meat and dairy products were his constant mainstay, and he continued to prosper, in spite of market conditions, while Amestoy and others were capitalizing on the boom in sheep raising. For several years the Plaza was something of a wholesale district, and Sentous conducted his affairs from rented quarters on Main. Later he bought the property, formed the Sentous Packing Company and erected the building that bore his name. Like Vignes, Beaudry, Marchessault, and many other countrymen, he was one of the numerous French people who made very notable contributions to the early life of Los Angeles.

When W.A. Spalding, one of the city's pioneer newsmen, first arrived in Los Angeles, March 1874, he found work as a reporter for the *Herald*. Theodore Clancey, the editor, allowed him to choose his own subject as a trial assignment. After a casual tour of the neighborhood, the sight he found most disturbing was the appearance of the Plaza, and he promptly wrote an editorial item calling attention to its "dismantled condition" and the need for improvement.

Originally only a barren field, the Plaza has undergone a number of transformations. At first it was merely an irregular plot of land bounded by adobes having little if any common alignment. Later it became a square, unkempt field with a gas lamp at each corner and criss-crossed by a number of well-worn footpaths. In the middle stood a large, unsightly, box-like reservoir. Some years later, when there was an awakening of civic pride, the Plaza assumed a more formal appearance. In place of the square plot there was a round expanse of lawn with a concentric arrangement of walks, encircled by a low ornamental iron fence. Around the turn of the century there were further changes, and Elijah Workman, with typical regard for the community, planted the trees whose grade canopy and boughs now spread over much of the Plaza.

Calle de los Negros, synonymous with all that was worst in the history of early Los Angeles, was located southeast of the Plaza. It was a passageway extending as far south as Arcadia, roughly parallel to the east side of present-day Los Angeles Street. At its northern limit it ended at a point where the entrance to Ferguson Alley was eventually located. Here, also, was the Plazuela, or O'Campo's Plaza; a rectangular clearing at the southeast corner of the Plaza, once famous for its cock-fights.

The view reproduced shows Los Angeles Street, looking south from the Plaza, before recent changes. In the early days, O'Campo's Plaza was located in the foreground, and the west side of the Calle de los Negros ran approximately in line with the edge of the curbing at the left. It was bounded on the west by the adobe dwellings of Don Francisco O'Campo and Don Ygnacio Coronel, which stood side-by-side in the area now occupied by the street, with the Plazuela on the north and the Coronel Adobe facing Arcadia on the south. Today, this section echoes to the drone of the freeway and there is no hint of its bizarre past or a time when it was the scene of one of the city's worst crimes, the Chinese Massacre★.

In the early 1870s, two of the chief Tongs were the Hang Chow and the Nin Yung. The

★After Hylen's original edition was published, the Chinese American Museum installed a commemorative plaque outside the museum entrance at 425 N. Los Angeles St. in October 2001. A larger memorial is planned for installation in the summer of 2026.

trouble began when a few young Chinese women arrived from San Francisco, and it was found that one of them had been given in marriage to a member of the Hang Chow. On October 23, 1871 there was a shooting in which their leader was attacked by one of the Nin Yung. In the midst of this fray a bystander was killed while trying to protect a policeman wounded in attempting to make an arrest. Shortly thereafter an infuriated mob gathered around the Coronel Adobe and began killing and looting indiscriminately. When it was over, eighteen Chinese people and one American were dead.

Eventually this area became the center of a fairly large Chinese community. For a while there was much vice and gambling. Neighbors protested but, as Workman said, stopping it was like

Ferguson Alley, looking east from Los Angeles Street
This photograph looks east on Ferguson Alley from Los Angeles Street toward Alameda. One can glimpse the entrance to Union Station and the gasometers beyond.

trying to sweep back the ocean with a broom. But in time it became a respectable part of the community. Ferguson Alley, connecting Los Angeles Street with Alameda, led to a neighborhood east of Alameda, where most of the Chinese population lived until the area was cleared for construction of the Union Station. The alley seems to have come into existence when the old adobes along Calle de los Negros were demolished. They were replaced by a row of two-story brick buildings used as business establishments by the Chinese. Years later, after an effort to convert it into a tourist attraction, it was destroyed and for a while, all that remained was the fragment of the southeast corner of Los Angeles Street at Ferguson Alley.

This neighborhood was once the main center of all celebrations and festivities in Chinatown and often echoed with the crackle of fireworks and the sound of boisterous crowds following the torturous movements of a paper dragon during New Year's celebrations. In fact, the Chinese contributed much of the distinctive color to the very popular Fiestas de las Flores during the nineties.

The west side of Los Angeles Street was the site of two other early buildings. One was the Ennette Block, on the northwest corner of Arcadia; the other, adjoining it, was built by Philippe Garnier in 1890. Abraham M. Edelman, the architect, was the son of the city's first rabbi. The Garnier Block, now the only one remaining, was designed particularly for the use of various prominent Chinese organizations. It continued to be used as such until the recent program of restoration began, still disclosing a few curiously figured signs here and there, so that an Eastern atmosphere lingered until the very end.

The panoramic view provides a visual recapitulation of most places thus far mentioned. All of the buildings on the east side of Main, from Commercial Street to the Plaza, can be seen. The

Above: Los Angeles Street at Ferguson Alley: southeast corner
Looking north; the balcony is at 434 N. Los Angeles St., from what used to be Calle de los Negros. Now it is the site of a Hollywood Freeway on-ramp.

Opposite: Garnier Block, looking north toward Plaza
The man in the white hat walks by the southern half of the Romanesque Revival-style Garnier Block (page 84); this portion of the structure was removed for the Hollywood Freeway.

Stearns Palacio and, later, Baker Block, stood where Main curves to the right. The Garnier Block with its large blank wall is clearly visible. Just above, on the east side of Los Angeles Street, is the Casa Lugo. Farther south, where the cars are parked, the north side of Ferguson Alley stands exposed. And the light strip of sidewalk nearby marks almost the exact spot where the Calle de los Negros was located.

South of this old section there was another area that figured very prominently in the city's development. It was roughly bounded by Main, Commercial, Alameda, and First and was for almost half a century the heart of commercial life in Los Angeles. During those years, these avenues hummed with activity and some of the liveliest traffic in the city. Before the Los Angeles & San Pedro Railroad was completed, stages from the harbor arriving via San Pedro Street veered left at a bend, later to be called Weller Street, before it crossed First and continued up Los Angeles

Above: Los Angeles Street at corner of Commercial
Isaias Wolf Hellman built the Hellman Block at the corner of Los Angeles and Commercial streets. It was designed by Ezra Kysor and built in 1871. Kysor, kept his offices here through the 1870s, until he designed and moved into a new block for Hellman on Main Street in 1882. The keystone windows and heavy quoining impart the solidity of a fortified Palazzo. The Hellman Block was demolished in mid-1963.

Opposite: Main Street, looking northeast from Commercial
Structures from pages 64–73 can be seen lower right; "SIGNS" is painted on the side of the Mercedes Theater (page 75).

Street. All this changed when the railroad was completed, initiating a boom and the greatest prosperity the area had yet known. Property values soared and, even years later, when the Salt Lake and La Grande stations began operating on either side of the river at First, there was an added impetus that continued well past the turn of the century.

The broad stretch of Los Angeles Street between First and Arcadia was the city's first center of commercial activity. According to some accounts, the Ord map erroneously assigned its original name, Calle Principal, to Main Street. However this may be, there seems little doubt of its early importance. Originally there was a continuous line of adobes along the eastern side, and Aliso was the only cross street running east. Commercial ended at Los Angeles Street. Later, when it was continued eastward, the extension was called New Commercial Street. Many of the leading merchants had large warehouses and offices on Los Angeles Street. Its unusual width gave heavy vehicles plenty of space to maneuver, while at the northern end, where the Coronel Adobe brought the street to a close, there was a spacious clearing with the large Stearns's Arcadia Block on the western side. A number of the old stores and warehouses remained until the area became a part of the Civic Center. One of the most well-known was that of Harper & Reynolds, just south of Market, with its entrance on Main and shipping dock on Los Angeles Street. Nearby, on the south side of Market, was another famous landmark, the Paris Inn. Although a relative newcomer, the Inn and

Intersection of Los Angeles Street and Commercial
Looking south on Los Angeles Street, the Hellman Block is at right.

its singing waiters will remain forever dear to Angelenos who remember the 1920s.

When the Los Angeles & San Pedro Railroad was completed in 1869, the terminal was located on the west side of Alameda between Commercial and Market Streets. Arrival of the boat-train was usually an exciting event. Carriages and omnibuses from the Lafayette, Bella Union, United States, and other hotels jostled each other for the trade. The Oriental Hotel, across the street at the southeast corner of Commercial, probably witnessed the excitement. Another relic of the prosperous era, dated 1885, stood on the northeast corner. West of it were several others, one of which later became the first Taix restaurant. Eventually the site of the terminal was bought by Isaac Lankershim and Isaac Newton Van Nuys, partners in the San Fernando Farm Homestead Association, for $17,500, to be used as the location of a plant for the processing of wheat.

On the east side of Main Street between Market and First there remained almost a solid row of buildings dating from about the 1880s. Of these, the Amestoy Block on the northeast corner of Market was the most impressive. The architect was A.C. Lutgens and it was completed in 1888. Fagan's Fountain was a popular hangout with the employees of city hall, just across the street. Another fine example of the same period,

Los Angeles Street, looking northwest at Market
The structure in the foreground, 201–203 N. Los Angeles St., was built circa 1885 and was the home of the J. M. Davis carriage repository. At left, facing Main Street, is the Amestoy Block. When these buildings were constructed, Market Street, running west from Los Angeles to Main Street was named Requena Street after Manuel Requena, who had served terms as Los Angeles mayor under both Mexican and American rule. The street name was changed in 1904.

Harper & Reynolds, and east side of Main Street

Harper & Reynolds, hardware merchants, built their new headquarters at 152 N. Main St. in the spring-summer of 1892. Architect Carroll H. Brown was well-known for his use of the Romanesque; his Harper & Reynolds Block featured carved Arizona sandstone. The Phillips Block—the white, thirteen-bay structure further down the street at 140–46 N. Main St.—was built in 1882 for Louis Phillips and designed by Burgess John Reeve.

The Paris Inn: 210 E. Market St.
The Paris Inn's original location was 110 E. Market St. from 1922–1930, before relocating a block east. The Paris Inn was designed in an eclectic half-timbered French style by architect Joseph Fosselman Rhodes and opened in March 1930. It featured a main dining room designed to look like a Parisian street in an "immersive experience." After this location was demolished in 1950 for construction of the Police Facilities Building, the Paris Inn moved to 845 North Broadway.

Joseph Mesmer's United States Hotel, once stood on the southeast corner. The career of Domingo Amestoy was a real-life rags-to-riches story. Born in France, he left home at the age of fourteen and came to California by way of Argentina and Cape Horn. Arriving in San Francisco while gold fever was still in the air, he finally found work at a sheep ranch after a brief try at mining around Tuolumne. When the flush days of sheep ranching dawned, his thrift and industry brought wealth. Later he became a charter member of the Los Angeles Chamber of Commerce and one of the original shareholders in both the Farmers & Merchants and Guaranty Trust & Savings Banks.

First Street had once been the site of many fine examples of early architecture, such as the Nadeau Hotel on the southwest corner of Spring and the Wilson Block, just opposite on the

Oriental Hotel: Alameda and Commercial
Originally known as the Alameda Building, the Oriental Hotel was built between 1888 and 1894. It was demolished in 1954 by General Petroleum to make way for a Mobil filling station.

southeast corner. Among the few that remained were the Pouyfourcat, J. & B. Wilson, and Gollmer Blocks. One of the most prominent was the Natick Hotel, originally the Natick House, on the southwest corner of First and Main, erected in 1880, three years before the Nadeau, at a cost of about $125,000. In comparison with the Nadeau, which cost nearly twice as much, it was less imposing and lacked the prestige associated with the many refinements of its neighbor, including the first elevator in Los Angeles. Originally the Natick was only two stories high, with a large porte cochère spanning its main entrance on the First Street side.

After redevelopment, the entire area east of the city hall was transformed beyond recognition. A series of four panoramic views, taken before all these changes happened, show not only its

Northwest corner of Commercial and Alameda
The Mott & Spence Block, at 601 N. Alameda St., was designed by the firm of Boring & Haas and built in 1885. It featured a full wine cellar and served as the headquarters for liquor and wine wholesalers Vaché Fréres & Co. and contained furnished rooms for rent on the upper floors. Now the site of the Alameda overpass, the Hollywood Freeway runs thirty feet below.

former appearance but the exact location of most of the buildings and places previously mentioned. Coupled with the view of the Plaza they form a sweeping panorama of nearly the entire area east of Main Street from Macy southward beyond First.

The first of the four views (page 104) shows the intersection of Los Angeles and Commercial Streets on the lower left. Commercial winds southeast to Alameda, in the center of the picture. Just across Alameda is the Oriental Hotel; another building previously noted stands across the street on the north side of Commercial. Opposite, on the southwest corner (beyond the hulking Los Angeles Warehouse), was the former site of the Los Angeles & San Pedro Railroad terminal. The majority of old places remaining along this section of Commercial were the last of a number that were erected during the flourishing days of the boom that began during the seventies.

Second in the series is a view looking southeast across First Street as it cuts diagonally across the middle distance from the right. The old orphanage once located on Boyle Avenue north of Seventh is dimly visible near the upper left corner. And running along the lower edge of the picture are some of the warehouses, built mostly before the turn of the century, that line the east side of Los Angeles Street north of First.

The third view shows the intersection of First and Los Angeles Streets, looking southeast. A continuation of the warehouses can be seen on Los Angeles Street. Catering mainly to various trades and industries, they extended about as far south as Fourth Street although, strictly speaking, such buildings continued many blocks further; as, for example, the garment houses between Seventh and Olympic. Historically, one of the most interesting details of this view is Weller Street, the short diagonal byway at the left, south of First. It was originally part of San Pedro Street, and

Above: Amestoy Block: South Elevation
The county turned the Amestoy Block into a parking lot in early 1959, redeveloped as part of City Hall East in 1973.

Opposite: Amestoy Block: Main and Market
Domingo Amestoy built a number of business blocks; one on Los Angeles Street near Requena (Kysor & Morgan, 1883) and another on Alameda (Kysor & Morgan, 1884). This block on Main was completed in 1887 and designed by Adolph Charles Lutgens, a San Francisco architect who kept a Los Angeles office during the 1880s building boom.

Overleaf: Buildings (126–134 N. Main St.) on east side of Main
134 N. Main St., left, dates to 1885; while the architect is unknown, the sedate Italianate form suggests the hand of Ezra Kysor. Right, the Morgan & Walls-designed McDonald Block, erected by Edward Nathaniel McDonald in 1892.

this intersection is where traffic from the harbor once came bowling onto Los Angeles Street en route to the center of town. Later Wilmington, which paralleled Los Angeles Street on the east, became part of San Pedro when the two streets were later joined between First and Second. Thenceforth the little diagonal stretch that had linked San Pedro with Los Angeles Street since the earliest days became known as Weller Street.

The series concludes with a panorama of the northeast corner of Main at First Street. It was one of the last groups of buildings to survive virtually unchanged since the 1880s. All of their neighbors across the street were demolished in the twenties to accommodate the new City Hall. Louis Lichtenberger's carriage works, a well-known institution in the horse-and-buggy days, was located about where the trees appear in the lower left-hand corner. Most of the buildings on the east side of the street are also shown at closer range. On opposite sides of First Street, at the top of the picture, the Pouyfourcat + J. & B. Wilson Building can easily be seen. A couple of "dinkies," the final type of one-man yellow cars before buses and freeways, are also visible near the intersection.

South of First, Main and Spring were for many years two of the principal business streets in Los Angeles. Even as late as the first years of the present century, they were the prime locations for the better hotels and commercial buildings. Today nearly all signs of that era have vanished. The railroad was still supreme, and most incoming traffic arrived via the Southern Pacific Station; when the men of Los Angeles returned from World War I the big parade was cheered along Fifth Street. The Alexandria (1906) and Rosslyn (1905) topped the local hotels and harbored the majority of visiting celebrities. Together with the Westminster and Van Nuys, they lent considerable prestige to the area. And in 1902 when Huntington decided to erect the tallest and

Pouyfourcat Block: 113–15 East First St.
Mary A. Pouyfourcat hired Abram Edelman to design this three-story business block, built in 1896. It was demolished in 1951 for the construction of the City Health Administration Building, along with the German-American Savings Bank, McDonald Block, and Harper & Reynolds.

LOS ANGELES BEFORE THE FREEWAYS

most expensive building yet built in Los Angeles, he chose the southeast corner of Sixth and Main. The two top floors were the home of the Jonathan Club, and it boasted the first roof-garden in Los Angeles. The roof also became a favorite vantage point for numerous postcard views of this newest part of the city.

But no one could foresee the swift changes ahead, and that these events were the last flowering of this once prestigious area. In the course of time, there was a steady shift in the center of activities, and signs of neglect and deterioration began to appear. Many of the smaller buildings south of First

J. & B. Wilson Block: 110–120 E. First St.
The husband-and-wife team of J. and B. Wilson built this block in the fall of 1891; its architect is unknown. The upper floors contained a forty-five room hotel, run by T. Henry Blewett, called Blewett House. The Wilson Block was demolished for a parking lot in 1958. The rubble in the foreground is where the Pouyfourcat formerly stood.

were either disfigured or destroyed to make room for parking lots. A typical example is the Robarts Block at the northeast corner of Seventh; it still exists, but in a condition no longer identifiable with the photograph. A few others, such as the one at 135–139 South Main continued in a sadly tarnished condition until the wrecking crew arrived. Also typical of the same vintage was the Weil Block across the street at number 148. It was the first home of the Security Trust & Savings Bank, which began operating February 11, 1889 in rented quarters on the ground floor with $29,000 in assets. First day deposits totaled $1,365. The cashier, later to become its president, was J.F. Sartori, one of the community's most outstanding business leaders. Sharing the building in those days was the Los Angeles Business College, with offices and classrooms on the second and third floors.

Further down the east side of Main Street, at the southeast corner of Second, is the Saint Vibiana Cathedral completed in 1876. Last rites for several early Angelenos were held here

Above: Natick Hotel: First and Main
This structure is known as the Bernard Block. It was built by John Bernard and designed by Burgess J. Reeve, and was completed in late 1882. Though designed as an office block, in March 1884 the hotel firm of Rowell & Dewing took over its lease, and redesigned the building for use as a hotel, naming it Natick House after Dewing's hometown, Natick, Massachusetts. John Parkinson remodeled the hotel in the spring of 1899, adding the third story and an elevator.

Opposite: Gollmer Block: 223 E. First St.
Charles Ferdinand Gollmer hired architect William Otis Merithew to design his 1888 Gollmer Block. At its right, housing the Atomic Cafe, is a two-story commercial project financed by prosperous lodging house owner Mary Wattell (also by Merithew and built in 1888). All were demolished in 1951 for the construction of the Police Facilities Building, renamed Parker Center in 1966.

LOS ANGELES BEFORE THE FREEWAYS

including Don Manuel Domínguez and Arcadia Stearns de Baker. On the latter occasion there were about 2,000 in attendance, including nearly eighty relatives. The church has been under the direction of some of the finest leaders in the spiritual life of Los Angeles. Bishop Amat, founder of the church, rested beneath the sanctuary until 1962, when a final entombment was made at Calvary Mausoleum. He had brought Vibiana's remains from Rome in 1855, but it was not until 1872 that work on the church finally got under way. The architect was Ezra F. Kysor, who had only recently completed the Pico House and Teatro Mercedes. The design was based on that of a Baroque-style church Amat had attended in Barcelona during his youth, and Kysor handled the task with characteristic ingenuity. But in the early 1920s, the façade was redesigned in a

Above: Panorama II: Area north of First, looking southeast from Los Angeles Street
The block in the foreground was demolished in 1951 for the Police Facilities Building. The Japanese Union Church (Henry M. Patterson, 1923) can be seen at center, at 120 N. San Pedro St. The majority of Little Tokyo was demolished and redeveloped by Japanese developers between 1970 and 1990. For example, the Civic Hotel, a center of Los Angeles Issei and Nisei life, was replaced by Kajima International's Sumitomo Bank.

Opposite: Panorama I: Commercial, looking east from Los Angeles Street
Commercial and Ducommun Streets led to the world's largest gasometer, a structure designed to store the city's supply of natural gas. The rigid, 377-foot tank was fabricated by the Bartlett Hayward Company in 1925 for Los Angeles Gas and Electric; to its right, a 1922 collapsible gas holder. By the 1970s, expanded underground storage facilities could handle peak gas loads; the familiar landmarks were dismantled in early 1974.

neoclassical manner by John C. Austin as part of a new master plan. The bell tower, however, was left unchanged; and this, as well as the entire rear elevation, is not only the finest feature of the church but one of the most exquisite pieces of early architecture in Southern California. Not so familiar was the view seen from Werdin place, a little-known alley threading midway between Main and Los Angeles streets as far as the south side of the church. Several of the buildings that once lined its course have either deteriorated or vanished.

Among the top dozen or more downtown hotels listed in a 1907 directory were the Natick and Grand Central (already noted) and the Westminster, which ranked among the city's most fashionable hotels during its time. Built by O.T. Johnson in 1887 at a cost of $231,261, it was the

Above: Panorama IV: Area northeast of Main and First
The building undergoing demolition at upper right is the Natick Hotel (page 103), demolished in the summer of 1950 for a parking lot.

Opposite: Panorama III: Intersection of Los Angeles, First, and Weller
Weller Street was renamed Astronaut Ellison S. Onizuka Street in 1987. The structures in the foreground were all demolished for the 1951 Health Administration Building.

Overleaf: Northeast corner of First and Main
The German-American Savings Bank, designed by Hugh Todd and completed in 1894. The bank remained at the location until 1907; in 1917, owing to anti-German sentiment the name was changed to Guaranty Trust, and eventually became Security First National Bank.

scene of many fine banquets and social events. General M.H. Sherman made it his permanent headquarters, and when Theodore Roosevelt came to Los Angeles in 1903 a great reception including the most important local dignitaries was held there. Even long after those days were gone, the ghost of its past still seemed to linger as one passed the entrance after dark, when the lights in the hallway continued to sparkle with a festive iridescence through the ornamental panes of its beveled glass door.

In the same vicinity there were a number of interesting places that have since been demolished. On little side streets, like Winston, there were unique relics, such as the Alcazar on the northeast corner of Main. While the main passenger terminals between First and Fifth were bustling with

Robarts Block: Seventh and Main
John Robarts was a prominent attorney (his partner, Henry T. Gage, became governor of California). Robarts hired architect John Hall to design his Robarts Block in 1888. It was demolished in 1958 and replaced with a one-story commercial building.

activity, much of the area east of Main was dotted with minor hotels and rooming houses. But with the decline of rail travel all these places rapidly deteriorated, until Fifth and its environs east of Main gradually became notorious as Skid Row, the first really blighted area in the city.

When Spring Street was in its heyday it was lined with Victorian elegance from First south at least as far as Seventh. Several landmarks, including the Nadeau and Hollenbeck hotels as well as the Wilson and Bryson blocks once graced the intersections at First and Second. Eventually most of them were razed and the *Times* building now occupies the former site of the Nadeau. Of the few that survived, two that faced each other on opposite sides of the street between Second and Third were typical examples. The latter of these stood on the west side, at the former site of the Turnverein Hall, one of the city's most popular meeting and entertainment centers during the 1880s.

On the northeast corner of Third and Spring, rising well above its neighbors, was the Stimson Building the first six-story edifice in Los Angeles. Thomas D. Stimson was a retired lumberman who came to Los Angeles and invested in real estate. The building, designed by Carroll A.

Left: Victorian Building: 135–139 S. Main St.
Percy Ripley Wilson, a successful attorney and the vice-president of the Merchants National Bank of Los Angeles, built the Wilson Block in 1887 using architect Burgess J. Reeve. At left is the Kurtz Block (Abram Edelman, 1886).

Right: Weil Block: 146–150 S. Main St.
Jacob Weil came to Los Angeles in 1850 and made his fortune in dry goods and groceries. He hired Abram Edelman to design the Weil Block, built in 1888. It was demolished for a parking lot in mid-1960.

Above: Westminster Hotel: Fourth and Main

Orson Thomas Johnson was a millionaire businessman and philanthropist who came to California from Ohio in 1880 and built a number of hotels and business blocks in Los Angeles. He hired Robert Brown Young to design the Westminster Hotel, which opened in early 1888. The Westminster is one of Young's better-known works, despite the fact that it was demolished for a parking lot in February 1960. The corner tower, bay windows, and mansard turrets made it a Main Street landmark for more than seven decades. This image dates to spring 1950.

Opposite: Werdin Place and Saint Vibiana Cathedral

In 1905, Thomas Higgins, a copper mine magnate from Bisbee, Arizona, developed the Bisbee Inn, "100 rooms on the European plan." Its architect was Arthur Leonard Haley. It still stands, having been renamed the St. George Hotel. In the distance, St. Vibiana Cathedral is visible.

Brown, was constructed in 1896 and helped substantially in providing jobs for those unemployed by the depression. The home at 2421 South Figueroa, where he lived from 1891 until his death in 1898, was also the work of the same architect. Its unusual woodwork, varying from room to room, and fortress-like exterior, became unique among local residences.

Farther west, on Broadway, the Bradbury Building is one of the most notable achievements of the nineteenth century. George Wyman's inspired combination of a restrained exterior with the surprising hybrid of imagination and utility that transforms its interior into a fantasy in ironwork still remains one of the finest relics of early Los Angeles architecture. Most of its contemporaries that once stood along Broadway, between Second and Third, no longer exist. Many of them are shown in the view of buildings on the west side of Broadway erected during the 1890s by J.W. Robinson and others. Robinson, who had first started business with the Boston Store on Spring near Temple, was considered rather brash at the time for moving, as it seemed, to the outskirts of town. No less historic is the parking area across the street. Along this part of Broadway the old city hall once stood at the left, and at the right (now marked by a plaque on the sidewalk) was the B'nai B'rith Synagogue, another of Kysor's designs. The immediate foreground was once the location of Turnverein Hall.

On both sides of Second, at the intersection of Broadway, were several other historic places. Around the eighties and nineties the entire area flourished and many new buildings were erected on the west side of Broadway between First and Second Streets. Most familiar was the Mason Opera House built in 1903 under the direction of Chicago architect Benjamin Marshall by John Mason at a cost of $163,347. With the turn of the century, the social climate in Los Angeles became more cosmopolitan and the Mason was a sign of the times. With the appearance of new luxury hotels like the Alexandria, Westminster, Van Nuys, and Rosslyn, and their elegant

Above: Alcazar Hotel: Main and Winston
James Boon Lankershim built this business block (Robert Brown Young, 1888) to house his newly incorporated Main Street Savings Bank and Trust Company. The floors above the bank contained a rooming house/hotel called the Menlo; Hylen calls it the Alcazar, which was its name from 1903–1910 (after which it was called the Royal Hotel). The Lankershim Block originally had a large corner tower—one of architect Young's architectural hallmarks. It was demolished for a parking lot in 1950.

Opposite: Victorian Building: 332–334 S. Spring St.
In 1888, Benjamin Cohen built the bay-windowed Cohen Block as the new home for his wallpaper and rug business. At left is the Willard Block (Carroll Herkimer Brown, 1893), a Romanesque Revival structure of rough-cut Lordsburg sandstone, built by WIllard Stimson. The Cohen and Willard blocks were demolished for a parking lot in early 1961.

LOS ANGELES BEFORE THE FREEWAYS

facilities for dining and entertainment, most of the more exclusive old institutions faded away. Organizations like the Cotillion and Chesterfield Clubs and their long-favored haunts gradually began to seem stodgy, if not provincial.

Unlike its predecessor, the Mason was designed to provide not only an ideal setting for the best in entertainment but a rendezvous for sophisticated theater goers. A major innovation was a spacious foyer where its audiences could socialize. Glancing through the old programs reads like a who's who of the theater during the first couple of decades of this century. Hardly a famous name is missing. George Arliss, Otis Skinner, Ethel Barrymore, David Warfield, and Walter Hampton were only a few. Managers and others were no less distinguished: Charles Frohman, Merle Armitage, and A.L. Erlanger were among the more memorable. Naturally, dining, dancing, and the theater parties became an important part of this entertainment, and old programs are filled with names of places then familiar to local bon vivants but now nearly all forgotten.

Conviviality and entertainment have always been a conspicuous part of life in Los Angeles. It is hardly by accident that it became, as it has often been called, the entertainment capital of the world. In the life of the *Californios*, fiestas and dancing were almost the order of the day. Possibly the birthplace of all ballrooms in Los Angeles was a plot of earth, packed hard as

Victorian Buildings: 215–219 S. Spring St.
Right to left: the Polaski Block (Abram Edelman, 1895); the Brode Block (Robert Brown Young, 1891); and the Romanesque Revival commercial structure at 221–223 Spring St. (architect unknown, 1889). Image shot in 1954; the Times-Mirror Company demolished the buildings for surface parking in early 1956.

LOS ANGELES BEFORE THE FREEWAYS

rock, once located at the southwest corner of First and Spring, now occupied by the *Times* building, where favorites like the vivacious *jarabes* and fandangos, with all their spectacular stampings and gyrations, were danced. But after the American occupation these carefree al fresco *bailes*, like so many other early customs, gave way to changing times. With the new arrivals came different tastes, and other dances like the waltz and quadrille took precedence. Saloons of every description flourished as never before, but as a more temperate way of life began to prevail, diversions more suited to the domestic temper began to emerge. Public gardens were specially favored, and George Lehman's memorable Round House and Garden of Eden on Main between Third and Fourth became one of the most popular.

Another was Phillipi's Gardens. Phillipi opened business during the eighties with a saloon in the Temple Block. It became a very popular place. Prompted possibly by the success of Lehman's Gardens, he decided upon a similar venture. However by 1879, after twenty years of successful business, he was beginning to experience financial difficulties. But Phillipi, intrigued by the possibilities of Fort Moore Hill and its long-famous view of the city, decided to go ahead with his plans. The Phillipi Gardens consisted of a spacious building surrounded by pleasant outdoor facilities and for a while enjoyed considerable favor as a local attraction.

In time the venture suffered a decline, but luckily for Phillipi, it caught the fancy of Mrs. Phineas Banning. Being a widow and alone with her daughters Mary and Lucy, she decided

Above: Bradbury Building: Third and Broadway
Two common misconceptions regarding the Bradbury Block are that its architect was George Wyman, and that Wyman managed to conceive of this absolutely unique structure as a mere untalented draftsman. In reality, the Bradbury's primary architect was Sumner Hunt; Wyman was supervising architect. Wyman was not a lowly draftsman, but a trained architect from the firm Peters & Burns. And the Bradbury, while an incredible space, was hardly revolutionary, being a lesser version of Eisenmann & Smith's Cleveland Arcade, which had opened three years prior.

Opposite: Stimson Block: Third and Spring
Lumber and banking magnate Thomas Douglas Stimson built the Stimson Block (Carroll Herkimer Brown, 1893) as the first six-story building in Los Angeles; it was also Los Angeles's first steel-frame skyscraper. It was the last major example of commercial Romanesque Revival in Los Angeles when it was unceremoniously demolished for a parking lot in July 1963. Stimson had hired Brown to design his Romanesque house on Figueroa Street, and Stimson's son Willard had used Brown for the Willard Block (page 22).

to have it remodeled and furnished it to become their home, which for many years remained a cynosure for some of the best families in Los Angeles. When those days were past, both the house and barn gradually degenerated into seedy apartment dwellings. Later the house was razed and only the barn remained. It stood on the east side of Hill Street, close to the steep declivity where the old concrete steps led down to Sunset Boulevard. Shown here is a view taken shortly before the building was demolished.

Not far from the Banning property was another long familiar landmark; the first Los Angeles High School, on the north side of California Street, slightly west of Hill. The architect was Ezra F. Kysor. Originally built on Poundcake Hill, at the southeast corner of Temple and Broadway, classes

Above: West side of Broadway between Second and Third
The structures across Broadway (from left to right) are the Boston Dry Goods building (Eisen & Hunt, 1895), the Newmark Block, also known as the Blanchard Music & Art Building (Abram Edelman, 1898), the Bicknell Block (Morgan & Walls, 1892), and the Potomac Block (Curlett & Eisen, 1890).

Opposite: West side of Broadway, looking south from Second
At far right, the eight-story Merchants Bank and Trust (Dennis & Farwell, 1905) still stands today, though it was reclad with a modern façade in 1968. At left are the Byrne Building and Million Dollar Theatre, at either side of Third Street, which remain standing. The block's other structures between Merchants Bank and Trust and the Byrne Building were either demolished for surface parking in 1953, or were cut down to one story and given blank façades.

first opened in 1873. The first students to graduate, numbering five girls and two boys, received their diplomas in 1875. During the boom of the eighties, the little clocktower courthouse on Main became inadequate for the purpose, so it was decided to move the school building from Poundcake Hill to make way for a red sandstone courthouse.

The next location chosen for the high school was Fort Moore Hill. This site was probably one of the most bizarre ever selected for a Los Angeles school. It was a clearing in the oldest nonsectarian cemetery in the city. Mountain man Andrew Whitley Sublette was one of the first to be buried there, and it became the last resting place of many well-known early Los Angeles residents. At the time when part of it was cleared to make room for the school, its condition had long been considered a local eyesore. Students later recalled eating their sandwiches and playing among the tombstones during lunch hours.

Only elementary classes were taught in the little frame building after 1890, when the brownstone and brick school was completed on Hill Street. The new high school, designed

West side of Broadway, looking north toward First
The building in the foreground at 109–11 South Broadway—advertising Rainier Ale and the 1952 Chevrolet—is the A.M. Hough Block (Bradbeer & Ferris, 1895); the entire block was demolished for the starkly modernist Junipero Serra State Office Building in 1955–56, which was itself demolished in 2006. The tall building in the distance, the Law Building (Taylor & Taylor, 1925) was the last privately owned building in the Civic Center, before it was wrested from its owners in 1964 and demolished in 1966.

LOS ANGELES BEFORE THE FREEWAYS

by a local architect named J.N. Preston, had many outstanding graduates. Susan Miller Dorsey, one of the most notable women in California education, was vice principal and later became superintendent of Los Angeles Schools. And one of its football teams won undying fame in 1898 when it defeated USC, 6–0. Strange to say, the wooden school outlasted its successor by several years. The photograph was taken a few months before it was razed. Another, on infrared film, defines it in sharper detail. In the panorama showing the southeast corner of Broadway and Temple, a part of Poundcake Hill, where the school first stood, is visible in the foreground; in the distance the school can be seen in its final location pending demolition. After it was demolished another view, looking opposite, was taken from a point close to the site where it stood, showing the extent of excavation necessitated by the freeway.

After the red sandstone courthouse, at Temple and Broadway, was razed in 1936, a number of temporary frame buildings were constructed in its place. The statue of Stephen White was left standing where it was first erected and later moved to its present location at First and Hill when the new courthouse was completed. Also left standing were the massive steps in rustic stone retaining wall around the old courthouse.

The Hall of Records, like its early neighbor the Courthouse, was built before New High Street was obliterated to make way for the new city hall and the northward extension of Spring Street. Consequently it was left standing at an angle that continually puzzled the younger generation. Even the old city fathers came to regard it as "an anachronism," which eventually proved intolerable to the fixed ideas of official thinking. Its architectural qualities somehow did not stimulate any interest.

The building, designed by Hudson & Munsell, was completed 1911, twenty years later than the old courthouse. In its way it was just as unique as the Bradbury Building. Its Mondrianesque exterior design, especially, was an exercise in the subtle organization of rectangular shapes that still seems quite superior to many of today's geometric exterior designs. Like the Amestoy Block, Casa Lugo, and others it should have been preserved at any cost; the best urban planners have generally agreed that such landmarks should be preserved as vital elements of the cultural background. But, as a *Westways* article regretfully commented "...we have once more lost touch with the past."

Still, it must be said on behalf of several civic authorities that serious thought was given to the idea of moving the building to face Temple. However, the estimated cost was prohibitive. And when the wreckers set to work, after all efforts to save it had failed, yet another architectural virtue was discovered; mainly its capacity to withstand extraordinary stress. Small wonder, then, that it stood firm during the severe earthquake in 1933 when the red sandstone courthouse was damaged beyond repair. Eight months were needed to tumble the walls, and toward the end "side-walk

Overleaf: Mason Opera House: 125–127 South Broadway
As a child, John Mason inherited a large fortune when his father passed. At age twenty-two, Mason put it all into a lavish, 1,600-seat opera house bearing his name; Mason Opera House opened June 8, 1903. Benjamin H. Marshall of the Chicago firm Marshall & Wilson designed the structure; the local supervising architect was John Parkinson. Its massive foyer was known for its thirty-foot Pompeian columns, made even grander in a 1924 remodel by the firm of Meyer & Holler. Frank Fouce took over in 1937 and ran it as a Spanish-language film and vaudeville venue. *Quinto Patio* on the marquee places this image in late-February to early-March of 1951. The structure to the Mason's north, near the right of the image, is the Newell & Rader block (Edward P. Carnicle, 1895).

superintendents" agreed that it was almost indestructible. Only the Paramount building at Sixth and Hill, constructed years later with much more advanced technology, proved comfortable in its resistance to the onslaughts of wrecking crews.

A different example, not far from the Hall of Records, was the State Building constructed at a cost of six million dollars and dedicated July 29, 1932. The building was designed for the use of Southern California judicial and administrative officials and their assistants. Its dedication attracted so much attention that all traffic at the Civic Center came to a standstill. Governor James Rolph, Jr., officiated and Vice President Charles Curtis of the United States was guest of honor. Highlight of the occasion was the presentation of the Distinguished Flying Cross to Amelia Earhart, honoring her two successful flights across the Atlantic. During the ensuing years the cumulative effect of earthquake shocks impaired the building's safety to such a degree that it had to be razed,

Banning Carriage House: Fort Moore Hill

Jacob Phillipi's saloon on Fort Moore Hill was called the Buena Vista; it opened in July 1883. Mary Hollister Banning, recent widow of Phineas "Father of the Port of Los Angeles" Banning, purchased the airy resort in 1887, and converted it into a fine home, which eventually became apartments. It was demolished along with the carriage house pictured as construction for the Hollywood Freeway advanced on the hill.

leaving only a flight of stairs leading to a view of its foundation, just across the street from the *Times* building.

During the first half century of American tenure, First Street slowly grew in importance until it became one of the most important cross-town thoroughfares. For several years the "junction" of Spring and Main at Temple had been the principal intersection of the central business district, but by the turn of the century the center of activity had definitely shifted south to the vicinity of First between Main and Broadway.

Bunker Hill was once an obstacle to the westward extension of several cross-town streets. First Street was one of them, originally ending at Hill. Later a cut was made, extending its route across the hill, and tunnels bored along North Hill, connecting First with Temple. The scars left by these massive changes at First and Hill can clearly be seen in the panorama. Steep bluffs remained at the

Original Los Angeles High School
By the 1940s, the school on Fort Moore Hill lay in the path of the Hollywood Freeway. After a protracted battle on the part of Los Angeles High School alumni to save the structure, the seventy-seven-year-old school was demolished in February 1949. Its historic entrance was saved and relocated to Los Angeles High School on Olympic Boulevard, through great effort and with terrific fanfare, and was then burned by vandals.

Fort Moore Hill and first Los Angeles High School from City Hall
The first structure on the lawn of city hall, next to the statue of Stephen White, was built in 1945, designed by J.F. Rhodes as dormitories for the United Service Organization, and converted to Superior Courts courtrooms and offices in 1946. Additional courtroom and office structures, designed by Edward C.N. Brett, were added in 1947. The statue was removed from the Civic Center and relocated to San Pedro in 1989. In the distance, upper left, one can view the encroaching Hollywood Freeway, which would slice through the hill and remove the high school.

LOS ANGELES BEFORE THE FREEWAYS

From the site of the original Los Angeles High School building
The view looking south on the Hollywood Freeway under construction, seen circa 1952. The Hill Street overpass is seen at center, with the Broadway overpass behind it. Adjacent to the Hall of Justice (Allied Architects, 1925) is the Hotel Alhambra (Peter August Westberg, 1907), converted by the county into a Hall of Justice annex until it was demolished in 1972. The dirt embankment at right is now topped with the Cathedral of Our Lady of the Angels, designed by José Rafael Moneo Vallés and opened in 2002.

ARNOLD HYLEN

northwest corner of Hill, as far as Olive on the north side of First, until the new court buildings were erected. During this period the entire east flank of the hill was leveled and a veritable mountain of earth was moved to provide space for the present-day mall.

In the panorama looking eastward along First from the bluff on the northwest corner of Hill, Boyle Heights and the Orphanage can be seen in the distance. The old police headquarters between Hill and Broadway is visible on the right. Two other views and taken from the western edge of the bluff encompass the vicinity of Olive at First. Continuing west on First there was an interesting variety of places adjacent to the present site of the Music Center. Like many of the colorful old haunts on Bunker Hill, these areas were like scenes out of the world of Raymond Chandler. Most of the inhabitants were quiet law-abiding citizens, the majority of them elderly, quite unlike some of the tense, lethal characters he liked to portray. If some appeared hostile, it was mostly because of the unsavory publicity that a few shallow reporters had begun to circulate. And while there were places that seemed to exude the hyped-up atmosphere dramatized by the writers, it was usually because the tenants

Old Courthouse steps, looking north on Broadway
Though the 1891 courthouse was razed in 1936, its steps remained, until demolished for the construction of the criminal courts building (Adrian Wilson, 1972). The Broadway-Temple Building (Walker & Eisen, 1926), left, was replaced by the Neutra-designed County Hall of Records in 1958, and the Women's Christian Temperance Union headquarters (Caukin & Haas, 1889, seen here after substantial remodeling) is now the site of the 1958 Central Heating and Refrigeration Plant.

Hall of Records and Former Site of New High Street
The Hall of Records (Hudson & Munsell, 1911) has an off-kilter placement, which indicates how New High Street once ran at an angle, before it was removed in 1928. The Hall of Records was the oldest civic structure in Los Angeles County when pulled down in 1973. Behind it, the tall structure is the Law Building (page 122).

Opposite: Hall of Records: North Broadway near Temple
The view from the Civic Center Plaza (now Grand Park). The Hall of Records displays its distinctly Beaux Arts arrangement of forms, with enameled brick and terra-cotta walls above a granite base, topped by swags and vaguely Flemish-Châteauesque dormers.

were too old or impoverished to improve their surroundings. Yet there were compensations. For not only did this spark the imagination of artists like Chandler and Joseph Losey, but their work, in turn, invested these surroundings with an aura of fantasy and bestowed on the hill and its inhabitants a permanent place in the life and literature of Los Angeles.

Many who crossed the stretch between Hill and Figueroa frequently seemed inclined to regard First as a boundary between two different hills. But even though there was no geographical distinction, the error was easily understandable, because the two sectors were quite different in some respects. The area north of First was comparatively isolated. There was less traffic and life moved at a much more tranquil pace. Hill Street Terrace, just above the southern end of the tunnels, and the cul-de-sac that was once Court Flight were almost unknown, except to the few elderly inhabitants who lingered there.

Hill Street, of course, has had a long and colorful history, but nearly all the remnants of its early days (and even many that were not so old) no longer exist. Latest of these casualties was the Bath Block, a long familiar landmark on the southeast corner of Fifth and Hill, demolished late in May 1980. Like its famous old neighbor, the California Club, that once lent dignity to the northwest corner, it has become a thing of the past; the 1904 structure was demolished in 1929 and replaced by the Title Guarantee and Trust Building, and the club built a new building three blocks west on Flower Street. So has everything that formally founded the intersection of Fourth and Hill, the next block north. For many years it was one of the busiest places in downtown Los Angeles, especially during the years when Arthur Letts first brought The Broadway department store to its earliest flash of prosperity. His career was one of the great success stories in local business, and when the store finally reached the limit of its expansion it extended along most of Fourth Street between Hill and Broadway, excepting a small section on the southeast corner. This was occupied by the Clarendon Hotel. In his biography, William Kilner fails to mention how Letts managed little by little to acquire all space adjacent to his first location without being able to include that corner. The fully expanded store, "an immense place, nine stories high, with entrances on three streets," opened on Monday morning, June 28th, 1915. Today it is virtually unoccupied and the southeast corner has become a parking lot. Another large edifice, the Black Building once stood on the northwest corner. Also gone is the quaint little cluster of buildings that once hugged the northeast corner, leaving the intersection more desolate than it has been for many years.

Angels Flight was beyond doubt without a rival among the city's most famous old landmarks. Ever since its inception, it had been a popular attraction, transforming Third and Hill from a quiet intersection into one of the most well-known sites in Los Angeles.

Until the end of the 1890s, Third Street veered south just west of Hill, following a stretch that was eventually to become the southern end of Clay Street. However it was then called Polyxena (an odd choice) after King Priam's ill-fated daughter. On Olive Street, just above a brush-covered slope, later to be cleared for the Flight and the mouths of Third Street Tunnel, stood the imposing

California State Building on First Street
The California State Building, executed in a monumental PWA Moderne style, was designed by John C. Austin and Frederic M. Ashley. Damaged by the 1971 Sylmar Earthquake, it was demolished in 1975, and has remained an empty lot since.

Bunker Hill at intersection of First and Hill
The First Street cut, which required the street grade to be lowered, occurred in 1894. The large parking lot on the bluff was the former home of the famed Bradbury Mansion, demolished in 1929.

LOS ANGELES BEFORE THE FREEWAYS

First Street, looking east from northwest corner of Hill

Four gentlemen gaze down at the intersection of First and Hill Streets. At left is the California State Building (page 137). Central Police State Division One (Charles Lincoln Strange, 1896) at 318 W. First St. was demolished in 1955. The Orphan Asylum (Curlett, Eisen & Cuthbertson, 1891), which Hylen mentions as looming on the horizon in Boyle Heights, was demolished in 1957.

Above: Olive Street near northwest corner of First
A mix of homes and wood-frame tenement structures. The structure at center bottom is 107–09 N. Olive St.

Left: Intersection of First and Olive, looking southwest
The Owens Apartments (James Lee Burton, 1904) on the corner was built in the fashionable Mission Revival style. The large structure in the background is the back-end of the Hotel Melrose Annex at 120 S. Grand Ave. (T. J. McCarthy, 1902). The entire block was demolished by the county in June 1957 to provide parking for the adjacent Civic Center.

Crocker Mansion. Below, along Polyxena, were a number of frame houses; the last one, much altered with time, stood at the old junction on the north side of Third.

Colonel J.W. Eddy, who built and managed Angels Flight for the first ten years, was a native of New York State. He was a close friend of Abraham Lincoln and also active in the presidential campaign. After serving in the Illinois State Legislature in 1866 and Senate in 1870, he came west to Arizona, where he spent three years supervising an extension of the Santa Fe Railroad south of Flagstaff. In coming to Los Angeles in 1895, he explored and surveyed the first projected route for transmission of water power from Kern River to Los Angeles. Later he became a member of the Los Angeles Chamber of Commerce. But his crowning achievement was Angels Flight. It was a precious legacy. Time can only enhance its memory and nothing will ever take its place in our affections.

The same must be said of Bunker Hill itself. It appears certain that as the inner city becomes swallowed up in steel and concrete, and men and women find themselves surrounded by blank walls, that the hill with its old-fashioned charm and intimate atmosphere, so completely absent today, will be missed increasingly as these finer values vanish from the scene. How deep-rooted this feeling is, can be judged from the fact that during one weekend alone, in May 1969, when the *Sinai* and *Olivet* were making their

North side of First between Grand and Olive
These structures along First Street were built mostly between 1899 and 1903. The block was completely demolished in August 1953 for the construction of the Los Angeles County Superior Court and Hall of Administration.

LOS ANGELES BEFORE THE FREEWAYS

final runs on Angels Flight, no fewer than forty thousand people came to enjoy a farewell ride.

North of Third on Hill there was little evidence of the past except the Vendome. Second Street, west of Hill, once a picturesque area, was the scene of some of the earliest signs of deterioration. The northern side, between Grand and Olive, was the first to be leveled. Looking westward across the empty lots, the backs of the Richelieu, Melrose, and other old buildings on Grand north of Second stood exposed in a lonely row. The south side of Second fared better. Everything remained untouched several years longer, including the Mission Apartments on the corner of Olive, the twin-peaked building at number 512, and the Dome on the crest of the hill at Grand Avenue. The Dome, originally called the Minnewaska, was the oldest and most visible landmark in that locality.

Olive Street was lined with a large number of interesting old buildings, mostly hotels. A block south of the Mission, at number 325 was the Ems. Looking deceptively small from the street, it was actually one of the largest on the hill, exceeded only by the Melrose Annex. Designed for a more humble clientele, this great box-like frame building was for many years among the best–

Left: Hill Street tunnels, looking north from First
Hill Street originally formed a dead end at this hill north of First Street. In 1909, the Los Angeles-Pacific Railway bored through the hill (the tunnel seen at left), continuing Hill Street through to Temple Street. In 1913, city engineers added an adjacent second tunnel for vehicular traffic. The tunnels were demolished, and the hill itself flattened, in 1954–55 as part of the Civic Center expansion.

Right: Terrace above tunnels, looking south on Hill Street
Pensioners sun themselves on the benches above the Hill Street tunnels as Hill Street stretches out beyond; First Street crosses below. A similar shot was captured by famed photographer Ansel Adams, shooting from the same vantage point.

Civic Center from top of Court Flight

A self-portrait; Hylen stands on Court Street east of Hill Street. At left is the Hotel Broadway (Carroll H. Brown, 1904) built by the father-son team of James and Avery McCarthy; the McCarthy Company founded the Observation Tower Company, which built Court Flight. Above is a corner of the United States Courthouse (Gilbert Stanley Underwood, 1940); the Hall of Records (page 132) and city hall. To Hylen's right, a thirty-three-unit apartment house called The Stevens (Harry Charles Deckbar, 1912). Hylen faces the dead-end where the Court Flight funicular (1904–1943) once had its engine house. Compare to the photo on page 136; Hylen is standing in that short bit of dead-end street.

ARNOLD HYLEN

LOS ANGELES BEFORE THE FREEWAYS

known hostelries on Bunker Hill. During its long existence it undoubtedly saw enough real-life dramas to provide many a Raymond Chandler theme. Most unique among this array of lodging places was a Victorian relic that overlooked the street from an aerie of palms and foliage behind a low wall of fieldstone at number 221. In Colonel Eddy's day it was no doubt one of the finer small residences. However in time the old place had degenerated into a rooming house surrounded by a thicket of neglected shrubbery.

But the street most notable for its hotels was Grand Avenue. From Temple southward, throughout the entire length of the hill, and even beyond, was once a continuous stretch of the city's best accommodations. Scattered among them were several fine residences, including the Rose Mansion. Their heyday spanned the 1880s and the turn of the century. Architecturally the hotels ran the gamut from classical columns to the conical roofs of Touraine, but the most elegant of all

Above: Black Building: northwest corner of Fourth and Hill
The gleaming white Black Building at 361 S. Hill St. was an eleven-story, 300-office business block developed by George and Julius Black. Designed by Edelman & Barnett, it opened in 1913 and was demolished by the Community Redevelopment Agency in January 1967.

Opposite: Bath Block on southeast corner of Fifth and Hill
The Bath Block (Robert Brown Young, 1898) was developed by Albert Leander Bath, vice president of the Stowell Cement Pipe Company. It was also known as the Hotel Willoughby, after Bath's mother's maiden name, Minetta Willoughby. The ogee arches lend a feeling of the Venetian Gothic. The massive electric billboard for Camel cigarettes, designed by famed advertising executive Douglas Leigh, included a small steam plant that blew "smoke" rings from the man's mouth.

was the Melrose. With its proud domes and ornate decorations, it was surely a crown jewel of the hill, and unique among the few remaining examples of the Victorian in Los Angeles. Many of the most notable personalities and events of the day were associated with its history, but when the end came it could not be saved for lack of funds, in spite of every effort to avert the loss. Finally vandals and fire solved the problem, condemning it to the same fate as the Dome in the Castle, among the hill's gallery of ghosts.

The next street west of Grand was Bunker Hill Avenue. While there were some who believe that it was named after the hill, the dilemma remains that among early residents it was simply another street in an area called Olive Hill. But regarding Bunker Hill Avenue itself there can be no question. It was the most quaint and memorable street on the hill. Its direct route, beginning at Angels Flight and continuing through its own little shopping center, at the intersection of Grand, led up to a steep little grade where Third Street came to an abrupt halt. This was the very summit of the hill and the heart of one of its most beloved and delightful little neighborhoods.

Bunker Hill Avenue will always remain the heart of the world of Leo Politi. Places identified with the writings of Raymond Chandler and Don Ryan tended to stress the seamy side of things. Certain aspects of the hill were sometimes used as props and, understandably, at times overdrawn to suit a plot. Specific places rarely emerge. But in

Northeast corner of Fourth and Hill
Originally known as the Stanford Hotel (and later the Brighton Hotel), its official name is the Strong Block, having been built by Austin F. M. Strong in 1895. Its architect was Frederick Rice Dorn. System Auto Parks engaged Cleveland Wrecking to turn it into a parking lot in July 1956.

Fourth Street at northeast corner of Hill

The view west on Fourth Street toward Hill, showing the south façade of the Strong Block/Brighton Hotel. At right was the Claremont Block (and a hotel called Claremont House) at 321–23 W. Fourth St., built in 1888. The "California Cafe" neon was fabricated by Artistic Neon and installed in August 1948. Both the Strong and Claremont blocks were demolished in 1956. The Black Building (page 145) can be seen across Hill Street.

LOS ANGELES BEFORE THE FREEWAYS

Politi's work one of the principal virtues lies in its fidelity to a time and place. Having spent a part of his life there, he was able to impart the essence of all that was most characteristic with incomparable felicity. The charm of its atmosphere and humble residents comes clearly into focus. Everything rings true, and those who appreciate his work may feel assured that this is how it was.

Many of the places that are mentioned here no doubt already become well-known to those familiar with his lively sketches. For them, the following views may have a two-fold interest, both as historic mementos and as the originals of Politi's colorful interpretations. It was fortunate that there were artists with the dedication and foresight to leave such an excellent record. Outstanding among the others is Ben Abril, who spent years putting many of the most typical scenes on canvas. Altogether, these spirited impressions in line and color have captured the quintessence of the hill in a manner that only the eye and imagination of an artist could achieve.

Politi called Bunker Hill Avenue the most picturesque street in the city. And, while some may demur, there can be no doubt that it was steeped in nostalgia. There was an exciting variety of places. Hardly a one was without some distinctive quality in appearance. Some of them were outstanding not only in design but because of their past associations. Among these, the Judge Julius Brousseau house at number 238, designed by R.B. Young in 1883, was certainly one of the most distinguished. It stood on a lot that sloped rather sharply toward Grand Avenue on the east, so that because of its advantage in height, it committed a fine view of the hill and its surroundings. The judge was the leading citizen and many notables were entertained there.

Just south of Third, on the opposite side of the street, were a few other places also destined to become a part of local history. The Foss home at number 315, dating from about 1885, was an ideal subject for any artist in search of the picturesque. Its weatherbeaten exterior seemed almost as much a part of nature as the luxuriant growth of shrubs and flowers that surrounded it. It was once as neat and trim as its neighbors, but for some unknown reason the owners did not interfere with

Angels Flight and Third Street tunnel at Hill
A later image of Hylen's, shot on 35mm film. This image was captured around 1962, after the Hillcrest Apartments at Third and Olive had been demolished.

Angels Flight, looking east on Third from Clay Street
A man walks the steps alongside Angels Flight—the city told its builder, James Ward Eddy, to include steps so the funicular wouldn't have a monopoly. In the distance, the tallest building (with cupola) is the Stimson Block (page 119), demolished in 1963.

LOS ANGELES BEFORE THE FREEWAYS

Clay Street, looking north from Angels Flight
The Sunshine Apartments building, at 413–23 W. Third St., was built at the end of 1904, architect unknown. Behind it, the rear of the Astoria Apartments at 248 S. Olive St. (Albert Julius Daniels, 1906).

Angels Flight and old house on northeast corner of Clay Street
Hylen did not live to see Angels Flight returned to Hill Street (a half-block south) in 1996. The mid-1880s frame house in the background, at 409 W. Third St., had once been the home of Rose McCoy. Originally located at the corner of Hill Street, it was moved a half-block west up the hill in 1905 when Rose's daughter, Catherine McCoy Stamps, built a business block on the Third and Hill site. The McCoy house was demolished in the fall of 1966.

LOS ANGELES BEFORE THE FREEWAYS

The Vendome: 231 S. Hill St.
The Vendome was built by Clara M. Praeger, widow of Dr. Emil Arnold Praeger, president of the Los Angeles County Medical Association. The architect was Charles H. Brinkhoff for the Barr Realty Company; it opened on New Year's Day of 1900. It was demolished in the fall of 1963.

Overleaf: South side of Second at intersection of Olive
At left, north of Second Street, a sea of parking lots after Los Angeles County demolished all structures in 1957 as part of the Civic Center expansion. The railing at center left tops the entrance to the Second Street Tunnel below.

time. Among the cinema enthusiasts it will always be associated with Joseph Losey's memorable remake of Fritz Lang's 1930 classic German film entitled *M*. It is a drama in which the city becomes a vital part of the action. Losey's version, made twenty-one years later, is an interpretation that ranks with the original. One of the major variations was the change of locale to Los Angeles; and among the most striking features of his film is the treatment of the background, in which the Foss home and its environment becomes as significant as any character in the plot.

A few steps farther south stood a place said to have been built around 1882 by one of Chicago's Armour family, and later acquired by D.F. Donegan. It was the last of the hill's famous mansions and probably more familiarly known as The Castle. Like the Foss home it was always a favorite among artists. This was the last house to be left standing on the hill, so to many it was not simply a matter of sketching, but an artistic farewell to a beloved place. And next door at 333 was a residence so well maintained that it seemed almost new. Only the design betrayed its age. But even in this respect there were few of the frills usually associated with the architecture of its day. Instead the ornamentation was largely confined to surface treatment.

Few areas of the hill were less known or frequented than the secluded stretch of Hope that dipped below its western flank, just above the mouth of the Third Street tunnel. Few except the older inhabitants knew about the steep incline with its scraggly growth of unkempt vegetation and

Left: Mission Apartments: Second and Olive
Harry Jackins built this sixty-four-room apartment hotel in the spring of 1905; it was originally known as the Jackins Apartments, then the Castle Craig when famed castle-building real estate man Alfred Guido Schloesser took up the lease. Post-1910 it was known as the Mission Apartments, after the style in which architect Arthur L. Haley designed it. It was demolished in mid-1964.

Right: Apartment building: 512 West Second
A structure of two flats, 512–514 W. Second St., built between 1888–1891. Through the 1920s and '30s it was known as the Chaspeak Apartments. It was featured in the 1962 motion picture *Days of Wine and Roses*, before being demolished in mid-1964.

the steps that led to a little cluster of stores at Flower Street. Politi fondly recalls how parts of this embankment were once terraced and planted with a variety of flowers and shrubs, since fallen into neglect. Farther south, at the intersection of Fourth, stood the Rev. Edwin Hildreth Mansion. It was the last survivor of the neighborhood that once bordered the little campus of the State Normal School, formerly located where the Public Library now stands. The most intriguing feature of the mansion, designed by Joseph Cather Newsom, was its ornate brickwork. It is interesting to recall that the corner where it stood was then one of the busiest on that part of the hill; and, that only a stone's throw east, at the corner of Grand Avenue, was the home of Leonard John Rose, one of the most elegant on the hill. When the Normal School closed the area declined. Beyond Fourth

The Dome: Second and Grand

James M. Shields designed and built the Mission Revival-style Minnewaska Hotel in 1903. Its Indo-Islamic dome made it a prominent signifier atop Bunker Hill, so much so that it was renamed The Dome in 1929. A deadly fire in July 1964 helped the Community Redevelopment Agency along with its pending demolition.

ARNOLD HYLEN

the hill blocked any further access to Figueroa as far south as Sixth; but part of the plan for the library involved the creation of a through street at Fifth. When the project was finished the old intersection of Fourth became isolated, and west of Hope it suddenly ended, leaving Hildreth's mansion on the edge of an embankment overlooking Flower Street.

Figueroa, one of the oldest streets in Los Angeles, seems to have begun as a trail. Originally the western slope of Bunker Hill was a long escarpment extending southward at least as far as Sixth. Together with a more gently sloping range of hilly terrain further to the west, it formed a broad ravine terminating in the vicinity of Olympic. Extending the length of this hollow, foreshadowing the course of the present freeway, ran Beaudry, Fremont, and Figueroa at ascending levels. The first two ended at Sixth, while Figueroa, joined by Flower at Second, continued directly southward. When work on the Harbor Freeway began, several blocks of buildings, ranging in size from small

Left: The Ems: 321 S. Olive St.
An 1883 house on this lot was removed in 1905 to where it stands today at 1032 Edgeware, in Angelino Heights. In its place, Charles Clayton Emswiler built the eponymous Ems Hotel, designed by architect Joseph Cather Newsom in Mission Revival style. The Community Redevelopment Agency hired Sav-On Wrecking to demolish it in the late summer of 1965.

Right: Victorian Residence: 221 S. Olive St.
Herman F. Baer built this house in 1887. It was designed by John Cotter Pelton Jr., a San Francisco architect who relocated to Los Angeles from 1886 to 1890, taking advantage of the housing boom. 221 S. Olive St. became a rooming house in 1905, and remained so until its demolition in spring of 1964.

The Melrose and Richelieu: 130–132 S. Grand Ave.
The Melrose (Joseph Cather Newsom, 1889) was built by retired oilman Marc William Connor. At right, the Richelieu, built as a hotel for and residence of Robert Larkins, a retired Chicago lumberman. The Richelieu's construction predates the Melrose by about six months, and was likely designed by Walter Ferris, then under the employ of the Newsom firm. Both structures were demolished by the County of Los Angeles in 1957.

colleges to a variety of hotels and apartment houses, standing along Beaudry and Fremont, all the way north of Sixth Street, were demolished during the process of construction.

This was for many years a pleasant little mid-town neighborhood. Numerous trees added a rustic atmosphere and there was even a miniature golf course for the local inhabitants. The area around Fifth and Sixth with the Jonathan Club and the tall spire of the Richfield Building rising above its huddle of old rooftops was the heart of one of the city's most charming enclaves. The Bellevue Terrace once stood there, and some years earlier the vicinity of Fifth and Fremont had been the location of the famous old Woolen Mill. B.F. Coulter, who later bought the mill, installed new machinery and continued operating it for several years. Water channeled from a local reservoir via the "woolen mill trench" was used to generate power and then allowed to flow southward where it served to irrigate adjacent farmlands. Figueroa was also the site of numerous hotels and rooming houses. Many had been razed to provide parking lots but a few still remained. One of the largest, the Monarch, appears on the left of the view looking east from Fremont. Diagonally across the intersection on the Southeast corner of Fifth, stood the Architects Building.

Looking west from Olive today, Sixth Street there is little if any resemblance to its recent past. Where there was once an almost unbroken row of small stores on either side of the street there is now only a canyon of monoliths. The little restaurants, grocery stores, and bookshop, with their

Left: The Brousseau Mansion: 238 S. Bunker Hill Ave.
Julius Brousseau came to Los Angeles with his family in 1877. He was a prominent attorney and, later, a judge. His ornate Eastlake-style home (Robert Brown Young, 1883) on Bunker Hill Ave. became a boarding house after the judge's death in 1903, and was demolished in late 1965.

Right: The Foss Home: 315 S. Bunker Hill Ave.
In 1909, a young mystic named Max Heindel met Miss Augusta Foss in the Foss family's boarding house. Discovering they had a penchant for esoteric theology, Heindel and Foss formed the Rosicrucian Fellowship together, a melding of Christianity and spiritual astrology, which today maintains thousands of adherents. Its headquarters are located in Oceanside, California.

intimate atmosphere and daily amenities, have given way to the routine formalities of modern business. The intersection of Sixth and Figueroa was typical. It has always been a busy place, even as early as the 1880s. The famous Bellevue Terrace once stood on the site of the Jonathan Club. The little streetcar line, of which Judge Widney was founder, also had its southern terminus at this intersection, with a service barn at the southeast corner.

Seventh Street, in the vicinity of Figueroa, is another scene of many recent changes. The new Broadway Plaza is probably more attuned to the needs of today, but it may still be open to question whether this commercial Kasbah has the charm and sophistication of the little row of boutiques. These exquisite shops, a section of the Martz Flats, were among the most unique of a number of interesting places that formerly encircled the block presently occupied by the Plaza. Among the most memorable were the old Y.M.C.A. building and Toto's restaurant on the Hope Street side.

Seventh and Figueroa is also much changed. The Barker Brothers building alone remains untouched. But the Paul G. Hoffman Studebaker sales room and garage has given way to the Hilton. The Zenda Ballroom, once located a block farther west at Francisco and long a popular rendezvous, has become a parking lot. Historically, the most significant spot was the site of the Hilton. Years before the Hoffman building was erected, the corner lot, a sloping tract of land that formed a hill extending toward Olympic, belonged to Samuel C. Foy. He was the owner of

Left: Victorian House: 333 S. Bunker Hill Ave.
This house was the home of Charlotte Temple Fraisher, likely built in 1890 by her husband Eugene Carberry, a carpenter, whom she married in January of that year. In 1901, it became the home of Spencer Roan Thorpe, a former Confederate colonel; his Louisianan wife hosted many events for Los Angeles's southern and French-speaking communities. After Thorpe's 1905 death, 333 became a rooming house, and was demolished in October 1966.

Right: The Castle: 325 S. Bunker Hill Ave.
Local capitalist Rueben Moore Baker built this house for famed Chicago meatpacking industrialist Philip Danforth Armour in 1887, though Armour abandoned his plans to live in Los Angeles and Baker became its first resident. He sold it to Daniel F. Donegan in 1894; Donegan gave 325 its "Castle" moniker.

a large saddle and harness shop, one of the city's finest, on Los Angeles Street, south of Commercial.

Seventh and Figueroa or Pearl Street, as it was then called, was at that time the center of some of the finest residences in town. Embowered among the flowers and shade-trees, and surrounded by spacious lawns, were the homes of the Tobermans, Perrys, Harolds, and Northams. Foy's property was then actually a hilltop and his home stood on the very crest. It was a large Victorian frame building with a fine two-story stable and carriage house adjacent. Topping it all was a windmill, spinning merrily in the breeze. It was rumored that his neighbors were unhappy when he failed to landscape his property, but Foy is reported to have answered that if God had wanted anything to grow there He would have ordained it. As a matter of fact, a contemporary photograph does show some landscaping, but it was hardly luxuriant.

This survey concludes with the end of the old neighborhood along Beaudry and Fremont and the beginning of the Hilton in the early 1950s. Fortunately, enough examples of each period remained during the years when this photographic record was being made to provide a fairly unbroken chronology before nearly everything had vanished. Several landmarks were excluded for lack of space. However there were a few that deserve special notice. One, the Rochester, was built in 1887 by Rufus Herrick Dorn to resemble an original he had seen and admired in Rochester, New York. It stood for many years on an embankment overlooking the south side of Temple, just west of the present Harbor Freeway overpass. In 1970 it began its sad pilgrimage to oblivion. After the house and truncated tower had stood side-by-side at Alameda and San Bruno for months, like a pair of derelicts, they were finally destroyed. Funds for the final stage of the scheduled journey to a haven at Heritage Square had somehow failed to materialize.

One of the other places stood above a very high retaining wall at number 835 on the north side of Sunset. Some details had been defaced by inept repairs, but its pervading charm remained undimmed in spite of the negligence. It was generally regarded as one of the best examples of Victorian architecture in America and often featured in books and news publications. The treatment

Above: Hildreth Mansion: Hope Street at Fourth
357 S. Hope St. (page 3) was built by Rev. Edward T. Hildreth, a Congregational minister, in 1889. The Hildreth became a boarding house in 1908, after the untimely deaths of the Reverend, his wife, and two children.

Opposite: Deserted gardens: Hope Street near Third
In this self-portrait, Hylen strolls north on Hope Street from near Third Street. To the right is 632 W. Third St., at the southeast corner of Hope and Third. Up the embankment, the backs of 251 and 245 S. Bunker Hill Ave.

Fifth and Beaudry, looking southeast
At the miniature golf course (page 184) near the corner of Fifth and Beaudry, looking southeast. The Richfield, a black-and-gold Art Deco tower (Morgan, Walls & Clements, 1929) can be seen at Sixth and Figueroa, along with the backside of the Jonathan Club (Schultze & Weaver, 1925).

Fifth and Fremont, looking southwest

At left, 545 S. Fremont Ave., a two-story residence designed by Morgan & Walls and built by Miss Cora Ellis in late 1904, which she converted to a six-unit apartment house in 1918. At right, the house at 533 S. Fremont was built by noted stamp collector William A.H. Connor in 1895. William Connor's father was Marc W. Connor, who built the Melrose in 1889 (page 159); note the difference a few years can make, in that the 1880s Melrose exhibited all the exuberance of the Queen Anne style, but a house built after 1893—when the Chicago World's Fair popularized neoclassical form—is designed with bilateral symmetry, columns, and a Greek Revival pediment. Both structures in this image were demolished about 1952 for the Harbor Freeway project.

Overleaf: Fifth and Fremont, looking east

At left, the Monarch Hotel (Cramer & Wise, 1929) was demolished in 1964, for the Union Bank Tower; the Architects' Building (Dodd & Richards, 1928) was demolished in 1968 for the ARCO Plaza towers. The two most prominent shorter towers in the distance are the Edison Building (Allison & Allison, 1930) seen between the Monarch and Architects, and to the right of the Architects' Building is the Central Library (Bertram Grosvenor Goodhue, 1926); those two, at least, are still with us.

East side of Figueroa between Fifth and Sixth
The Bur-Mar Hotel (William H. Enders, 1903) with the tall Corinthian columns, stands at 514 S. Figueroa St. Its darker neighbor at 516, a twenty-one-room apartment house called the Saint Dunstan, was built in 1904. They were both lost to a surface parking lot in 1957. Looming behind is the Richfield Tower (Morgan, Walls & Clements, 1929). The Richfield was demolished in 1968 for the ARCO towers project, along with the rest of its block.

of the verandah was especially interesting and much admired by students of period design. Not quite so well known, but in some respects even more exquisite was another house that stood on the west side of Bixel, just north of Seventh. The intricately related details of carving, wrought-iron, and stained glass throughout ranked among the best local examples of that era.

Nearly all of the most unique relics have disappeared. Now only Carroll Avenue and a few other isolated places remain. On July 15, 1980 the city's Public Works Bureau of Engineering initiated a five-year program to make a historical survey of "close to a million individual parcels within the city's approximately 468 square miles." This is surely an ambitious and commendable project, and, even though so many memorable landmarks no longer exist, it is reassuring to know that a significant part of our more recent heritage faces better prospects.

Since this is essentially an informal account of first-hand observations, no historical references have been listed. Original usage has been respected. Filipe de Neve did not sign his name with an F, nor was "*Nuestra Señora*" omitted from the name of the Plaza Church. They are redolent of the past and, right or wrong, the older natives commonly spoke of "*Casa Lugo*," "*Teatro Mercedes*," and so on. No other words to convey the atmosphere of early Los Angeles more vividly than these germane antecedents, and they should be exempt from scholarly dogma. Most of the other information is already fairly common knowledge but, whatever the case, all facts have been carefully checked. No less valuable have been the many enlightening comments garnered from numerous conversations with Robert F. Scherrer and Ernest C. Kennedy.

Left: North side of Sixth at corner of Figueroa
The laundry/shoe repair is 823–25 W. Sixth St. (Kremple & Erkes, 1912), books/magazines is 827–829, built as the Star Theatre (Lester Sherwood Moore, 1914), and the Hotel Clinton on the corner was put up in late 1902, architect unknown.

Right: Northeast corner of Sixth and Figueroa
The Hotel Clinton at 554 S. Figueroa St. was turned into a parking lot in late 1955, and remained one until the construction of the ARCO towers on the site.

Boutiques at Martz Flats: Seventh and Flower

Henry Martz built the Martz Flats in 1895 as a row of ten houses in flats, at the corner of Seventh and Flower Streets. Though the architect is unknown, in all likelihood Julius Krause designed it, as Krause also designed a business block for Martz on the 400 block of Broadway in 1898.

LOS ANGELES BEFORE THE FREEWAYS

Seventh Street, looking east at Figueroa

At left is the Harold L. Arnold Building (Thomas Beverley Keim, 1922), an automobile showroom and service building, seen here as the home of Hoffman Studebaker. The sign reads "Removal Sale" because the building would soon be demolished for a new Statler Hotel (page 175).

ARNOLD HYLEN

PHOTOGRAPHY IN LOS ANGELES

The beginnings of photography in Los Angeles very nearly coincide with the incorporation of the city itself. According to the best information available, Dr. William S. Osborne and Moses Searles, two local amateurs, are believed to have taken the first local daguerreotype on August 9, 1851. Other daguerreotypists of the same period were Messrs. Carvallo & Johnson, about whom very little is known, and Henri Penelon. Whether any of these pioneers ever did anything except portraits seems doubtful. Penelon, of course, will mainly be remembered for his decorations at the Plaza Church and, most notably, his memorable series of paintings of the early Dons and their families.

In spite of this precedence in time, a number of years elapsed before photographers made any effort to record the city. A few, including Edward Vischer and William Godfrey, appeared to have been doing so as early as the 1860s. Among the later photographers there was one in particular who dedicated most of a lifetime to the pictorial documentation of Los Angeles and its environs. Both the man and his efforts have long been overlooked. His name was Charles C. Pierce. He began working around the city

Seventh Street, looking west at Figueroa
A reverse view of the previous image. The banner welcomes Atlanta's Yaarab Shrine to the Shriner's Convention of June 1950, whereby 135,000 Shriners packed Los Angeles. The "Samsonite" building, left, was built as a Hellman Bank (Walker & Eisen, 1920); it was demolished for a Union Oil service station in 1956.

about 1886. Noah never labored with greater devotion. Far from being confined to his own work this endeavor included a lifelong effort to assemble an archive of the work of all his predecessors. His own photographs of Los Angeles apparently covered a period of more than forty years, ending around 1930.

The bulk of his collection was eventually acquired by the Title Insurance Company and reproduced quite extensively in books and pamphlets written by W.W. Robinson, as well as numerous other historical publications. Lately most of these photographs and negatives were generously donated to the California Historical Society. The Huntington Library also acquired a sizable part of the collection, while other institutions shared the remainder in varying portions. Altogether it represents the most important and voluminous contribution ever made to the photographic annals of Los Angeles and Southern California.

Much credit is due to the California Historical Society for its articles in recognition of such men as Muybridge and Watkins, and California photography in general. The comments regarding Pierce by Gary F. Kurutz in the summer issue of the 1978 *Quarterly* were eminently noteworthy,

Beginning of the new: The Hilton and Freeway from Sixth and Flower
This 1951 image looks south across West Sixth Street; the construction at foreground is an off-ramp of the Harbor Freeway. At left, the back of St. Paul's Cathedral (Johnson, Kaufmann & Coate, 1924), demolished 1980. The steel skeleton at Seventh and Figueroa is the Hotel Statler (Holabird, Root & Burgee, 1952), which replaced the Studebaker dealership (page 171). The Statler, later a Hilton, an Omni, and finally the Wilshire Grand, was demolished in 2013.

especially since the recognition has been so long overdue. As Kurutz says, the history of photography in Los Angeles has been "scantily documented." This is regrettable. For while the origins were humble, the historic moments captured in these routine images form a priceless record of the past. Their value exceeds all technical criteria; and many of those who tripped the shutter, talented or not, have merited something better than years of neglect.

The importance of accumulating a historic record in words and pictures has long been recognized by local groups. But to date, as the foregoing proves, the task has always fallen into the initiative of a few isolated individuals. As early as 1895 Edwin Baxter was concerned about the problem. Speaking to members of the Historical Society of Southern California, he stressed the importance of documentation, and cautioned that the lasting importance of any first-hand record, however trivial it might seem, could only be determined by posterity. He emphasized the fact that their main objective is simply to ensure the "perpetuity" about aspects of our community from generation to generation. A reaffirmation came years later, in 1958, when Lawrence Clark Powell spoke of the "great lineage" in his memorable address, "The Sense of the Past," repeated Baxter's message with added emphasis. With equal foresight he admonished, "We should employ a photographer to do nothing but photograph the local scene, day after day, of one street, down another, recording the present before

Above: Victorian Residence: Bixel north of Seventh

Peter Wilson, a Swedish sailor, came to Los Angeles in 1851. He prospered in real estate, and in 1882 hired Kysor & Morgan to build a fine house at 532 S. Spring St. Wilson passed in 1886, and in 1895 his widow Catherine moved the house from the urbanizing downtown to "far-flung" Seventh and Bixel Streets. The structure stood at 1103 W. Seventh St. until it was moved one lot north by owner Nicola Bonfilio (director of the Bank of Italy) in 1922, when Bonfilio built a commercial structure on the corner. The old Wilson house remained at its new location on 691 S. Bixel St. until it was demolished in the fall of 1956.

Opposite: The Rochester, 1012 W. Temple St.

The Rochester House and Cottage, with its mansard roof, was designed in Second Empire style by the team of Rufus Herrick Dorn & Albert Gardner Slocum. Dorn's son, Frederick Rice Dorn, became a noted architect. The Rochester was declared a Historical-Cultural Monument in 1963. The El Pueblo de Los Angeles State Historical Monument Commission raised money for its restoration, and arranged to relocate it to a surface parking lot at the southwest corner of Main and Republic Streets. Moved to a "temporary site" at Alameda and Bruno Street in September 1970, it languished, and was demolished in February 1979. Its proposed relocation site remains a parking lot.

it is lost to view. Southern California has many beautiful backwaters, unknown to or disregarded by the chamber of commerce. Dare I speak of Bunker Hill?"

The task, of course, is never-ending. Now that nearly all of early Los Angeles is gone, time is beginning to overtake the world of the twenties and thirties. Nowadays the young look upon art deco in much the same way as their elders once regarded things Victorian. Several fine examples are among the places being threatened by change. A book might be devoted to the Oviatt Building alone, so characteristic of its period and design and exquisite details of wrought metal and Lalique glass. And hidden away in different neighborhoods are numbers of old bungalows and dwellings harking back to the days when there were no freeways and life moved at a much more leisurely pace. To any who still remember those times, the city remains full of nostalgic byways. Elderly citizens who lived here when the tomb of King Tut was discovered, and Egyptian motifs became a rage in everything from fashions to architecture, might be pleasantly surprised to find such relics as an apartment building in the shape of a temple on the Nile, still lingering on a side street off Olympic.

Odd as it seems, these places now have become our oldest links with the past. Nearly all that antedated them is virtually gone. They have become symbols of a time when the city had lost its Victorian character and begun to develop a personality of its own. When a war-weary public succumbed to the fantasy world of Fairbanks and Valentino, local architects fell under the romantic spell of Hollywood, culminating in a variety of plaster adaptations such as the Garden of Allah and Falcon Lair. Art Deco also enjoyed a few short years, during which it seems the ultimate in avant-garde. Some called this the age of Stucco. It was a time that should provide a wealth of material for the historical projects now being initiated. Modern techniques of documentation, especially in photography, have advanced so greatly since the days of Pierce and his contemporaries that the present generation seemed certain not only to provide a worthy sequel to the chronicle of these pioneers but one that will enhance the tradition they have established.

Most of these views were taken between the early 1940s and 1960s. That was virtually the swan song of early Los Angeles. And while it remained there was, fortunately, time enough for a last long parting look.

End of the old: The Castle on Bunker Hill Avenue
Here, the Castle (page 161) has had its surroundings demolished. Behind the Castle to the left, a glimpse of the Salt Box. The Castle and Salt Box were the sole Bunker Hill homes saved by the Department of Recreation and Parks and moved to a new museum of Los Angeles's Victorian past called Heritage Square in March 1969. Both structures were burned to the ground seven months later.

Looking north on Hill, toward Second Street.

A stroll on Hill Street toward the intersection of Second. It had recently rained, and there were cocktails to be had in the Astor Hotel bar. In the distance, the Hill Street tunnels, and above, the Moore Cliff apartments. By the end of 1956, the hill that contained both would be wiped away, to provide a clean slate for the county courthouse project.

Opposite: The Johnson Block/Westminster Annex

O.T. Johnson built 121 E. Fourth St. in 1894 as an annex to his Hotel Westminster (page 113). Like the 1888 Westminster, it was designed by Robert Brown Young. It was demolished for a parking lot in 1952.

691 S. Bixel St.
The original edition featured a detail of the Wilson house on Bixel (page 177) but Kysor's 1882 structure deserves to be seen in its entirety. It reads as classic Eastlake, via its board cladding and symmetry; the naturalistic applied vine ornament is a particularly Eastlake touch. And yet it has canted bays as opposed to square, and is leant asymmetry via the differentiation of its gables and offset porch. It verges into the Queen Anne through the profusion of carving, inclusion of stained glass, and fishscale shingle.

LOS ANGELES BEFORE THE FREEWAYS

Chavez Ravine

Hylen did not write about Chavez Ravine, but he did venture there. He stood atop Mount Lookout, facing northwest; the paved street below him is Bishops Road. The two main trails that form a "V" run up to Pine and Spruce Streets, in the neighborhood of Palo Verde. The homes in Chavez Ravine were taken by the Housing Authority of the City of Los Angeles via eminent domain and demolished in 1951–53.

Golfing Downtown

The 1920s saw a craze for miniature golf, though most courses closed at the outset of the Depression. 1937 saw an upswing in interest, as the Gittelson Brothers built new courses across town, including a $100,000 facility with two eighteen-hole greens bounded by Fifth, Fremont, Beaudry and Maryland (page 164). It was demolished in 1951. The two most prominent structures in the distance, the Architects' Building (Dodd & Richards, 1928), left, and the Richfield Tower (Morgan, Walls & Clements, 1929), right, were both demolished in early 1969.

Nearing the End
One of Arnold Hylen's final photographs, shot on 35mm during a trip downtown in July 1979. Looking west on Third across Hill Street—where Angels Flight once ran up to Olive Street, the hill has been flattened; compare to (page 149). The construction underway is for the Angelus Plaza retirement complex. A new presence on Bunker Hill, the Security Pacific Bank (A.C. Martin Associates, 1974) at Third and Hope Streets, looms above.

AFTERWORD

It was 1993. I was living in Wisconsin, finishing my master's degree at UW Madison, on the brink of PhD work in architectural history. But I began reading Raymond Chandler and James Ellroy and their ilk, at which point I dropped academia and moved to Los Angeles. I bought a 1949 Packard and headed out into the night in search of the postwar world of ancient, decaying LA.

I caroused and prowled the city, and in my travels was repeatedly told there were a couple books I absolutely required: back in the 1950s some photographer had driven around Los Angeles, capturing this landscape I now romanticized and fetishized, a vanished downtown replete with ramshackle Victorian houses and cast-iron commercial structures, where disreputable detectives drowned their sorrows in cinematically smoke-filled chop suey joints. That photographer's name was Arnold Hylen and his two books—the 1976 *Bunker Hill: a Los Angeles Landmark* and 1981's *Los Angeles Before the Freeways*—were, I was assured, the best vehicle by which to understand archaic Los Angeles. Apparently they featured incredible pictures and text, but were maddeningly rare: they had very limited print runs, and collectors snapped up what few copies existed.

I would search for these two books on Bookseller's Row, along Sixth Street, and among the bookdealers on Grand Avenue near Fifth Street. At last I came upon copies of both, bit the bullet, and spent that month's rent on the pair. I was now in rarefied company, both as owner of the books and more importantly, now armed with an understanding of downtown's built environment both visually and via an explication of its development; I was able to time travel through its streets and alleys with ever-increasing insight.

Eventually, Hylen's images crept up on the internet (he gifted some prints to the California State Library in Sacramento in 1985, which put them online about 2005). But the library's

uploaded images, by themselves, lacked context—specifically, Hylen's text—and I began giving thought as to how I might manage republishing his books to reach a wider and rightful audience.

The road to acquiring publishing rights, and the original negatives, was demanding. It took some years of locating, contacting, and working with remaining members of the family. Lawyers were engaged, contracts signed, and I had to sell the Packard to fund purchase of the materials, but at last I acquired the rights and negatives to both books. It was only then I was informed the vast archive relating to *Bunker Hill, A Los Angeles Landmark* had been lost.

The loss of the negatives for Hylen's *Bunker Hill* book meant that that could not be republished, so I directed my energies into the production of a larger book about Bunker Hill, which utilized some Hylen images and quoted him at length. My book *Bunker Hill, Los Angeles: Essence of Sunshine and Noir* was published by Angel City Press in 2020. The *Bunker Hill* book completed, I turned my attention to the republication of Hylen's *Los Angeles Before the Freeways*. In doing so, I hope to deepen our collective awareness and knowledge surrounding the built environment of Los Angeles's formative years, which we have so casually and callously discarded. The photography and text of Hylen's book is arguably the best record of old Los Angeles ever made, hence my need to republish the book you now hold in your hands. I hope it becomes as meaningful for you today as it did for me thirty years ago.

—*Nathan Marsak, 2025*

Above: The original 1981 edition of *Los Angeles Before the Freeways*.

Overleaf: Left to right: Downey Block, Grand Central, Pico's Building, and the former site of Bella Union. Pico's Building (at right) was built by Pío Pico in 1868, two years before he built Pico House.

About the Authors

Arnold Hylen (1908–1987) trained at the Chouinard Art Institute, and found work as a photographer for the Fluor Corporation, where he worked from the early 1940s into the 1970s. During that period, he spent his free time photographing vanishing old Los Angeles. Hylen compiled his work on the downtown neighborhood of Bunker Hill in *Bunker Hill: A Los Angeles Landmark* (1976) and his research on greater downtown in *Los Angeles Before the Freeways 1850–1950: Images of an Era* (1981)

Nathan Marsak studied under Reyner Banham at the University of California, Santa Cruz, and completed his graduate work at the University of Wisconsin, Madison. He worked on the curatorial staff of Los Angeles Museum of Contemporary Art and served as historian for the Los Angeles Police Museum archives. His books are *Los Angeles Neon* (2002), *Bunker Hill Los Angeles* (2020), *Bunker Noir!* (2021) and *Marsak's Guide to Bunker Hill* (2023).

Acknowledgments

Great thanks go out to Terri Accomazzo at Angel City Press, who believed in this project. Kudos as well to ACP's incomparable book designer Eric Lynxwiler.

The republication of this book would not have been possible without Arnold Hylen's grandniece Lisa Siddens, who stored the *Freeways* archive after her great uncle's death, and from whom I purchased the material.

As always, everything is due to my wife Nicole, who supports me unreservedly.

Victorian Residence: 835 W. Sunset Blvd.
Coffee and tea merchant Mechaelis "Michael" T. Herzog came to Los Angeles from Prussia in 1875 and built this house in 1892. Though its architect is unknown, given its multiplicity of surface elements—and inclusion of an "Eastern" faceted dome over a cusped arch, atop a Chinese moon gate—the easy attribution would be Joseph Cather Newsom, though Newsom had moved to San Francisco in 1890; the likeliest candidates for attribution are James H. Bradbeer, or the firm of Merithew, Ferris & Creighton. It was demolished in May 1961.

LOS ANGELES
BEFORE THE FREEWAYS

IMAGES OF AN ERA 1850–1950

By Arnold Hylen with Nathan Marsak

Photographs by Arnold Hylen

Copyright © 2025 Nathan Marsak

Design by J. Eric Lynxwiler, Signpost Graphics

10 9 8 7 6 5 4 3 2 1

978-1-62640-133-4

Library of Congress Cataloging-in-Publication Data is available.

Published by Angel City Press
at Los Angeles Public Library
www.angelcitypress.com
Printed in Canada

The Hall of Records
The endpapers reflect the cover for Hylen's 1981 edition of *Los Angeles Before the Freeways* (page 187). Hylen captured this image of the Hall of Records (page 132) circa 1962.